Summer Snow

Summer Snow

NEW POEMS

Robert Hass

ecco

An Imprint of HarperCollins*Publishers*

HarperCollins books may be purchased for educational, business, or sales pro-
motional use. For information, please email the Special Markets Department at
SPsales@harpercollins.com.

FIRST EDITION

Designed by Joy O'Meara

Library of Congress Cataloging-in-Publication Data has been applied for.

ISBN 978-0-06-295002-4

20 21 22 23 24   LSC   10 9 8 7 6 5 4 3 2

For Brenda

Contents

FIRST POEM

In the dream he was a hawk with blood on its beak.
In the dream he was a hawk.

In the dream he was a woman, naked, indolent from pleasure, a gleam of
    sperm on her vaginal lips.
In the dream he was a woman.

(He could both be the woman and see the viscid fluid in the dream.)

In the dream he was a turquoise bird fashioned from blue stone by a
    people who dug it from the earth and believed it was the shattered sky
    of a foreworld.
In the dream he was the turquoise bird.

In the dream his feet hurt, there was a long way still to go, lizards
    scuttling in the dust.
In the dream his feet hurt.

In the dream he was an old man, his woman gone, who woke early each
    day and made his pot of coffee and sliced bits of melons for the lizards
    and set them on the hard ground by the garden wall.
In the dream he was the old man.

The calm mouths of the lizards as they waited, themselves the color of the
    dust, meant that every creature was singular and solitary on the earth.

In the dream the woman in the elevator took out her eye.
It was a moon in the dream.

In the dream there was a knock on the door and it was the troop of
begging children and he said to them in mock outrage, "You! Scoot!
This is not your day. Tuesday is your day," and the children laughed
with great good humor.
Their day was Tuesday in the dream.

NATURE NOTES IN THE MORNING

After days of wind,
No wind.
The leaves of the aspen are still.
The leaves of the alder and cottonwood,
Juddering for days and cold,
Are still.

———

East sides of the trees
Are limned with light.
Last night a stand of lodgepoles
Lit on the west side.
A kind of symmetry in days
Because they're standing still.

Just distribution theory:
Light.

———

What do I know from yesterday?
The blue bell of the gentian on the trail.
Hawk moths swarming in the scree.

Two drops of violet
In a pool of azure:
Petals of the gentian.

———

The leaves lit by light,
The rock face of the mountain gleaming.

—

And only for a second yesterday
The tanager's yellow breast.
As if the gift were excessive.

I marked the gentian's location:
At a turn in the trail, left side going up.
Right side coming down, fern shading it,
Incense cedar above it, two boulders
Of granite, mica-flecked, and I still couldn't find it
On the way back down.

—

Itō Jakuchū smeared a paste of egg yolk
And white paint on the back of his scrolls
And then crushed oyster shell to another paste
And added carmine for the rooster's crest
He painted into the soft silk.

Smuggled Prussian blues from Europe
(There was a Tokugawa trade embargo)
For the way light looked on plums.

—

Values in the right place: a country
That outlaws the use of Prussian blue.

—

Lists of colors to ban from future kingdoms:
(Make list here.)
(Terre verte, alizarin.)

—

Lips: carmine.
Last streaks of sunset: alizarin.

—

The old art historian. I was going on
About Cézanne and he took me into the studio
And took down four tubes of shades of green
And stood me in front of an easel with a brush
And said, "Now, put these on paper
In small rectangular daubs so that they shimmer,
And until you can do that, I say this
In all friendship, shut up about Cézanne."

—

That was—what?—forty years ago.
Professor Henry Schaefer-Simmern.
Trained at Bauhaus. Escaped the Nazis in 1939.
He wore bow ties and plaid shirts, wrote about perception.
Big man, full of vitality.
He must be long dead.

—

Sierra morning.
Bright sun. No wind,
So that stirring in the cottonwood
Must be a warbler.

SPREZZATURA

Eugenio Montale asked me if there was an American word
For *sprezzatura,* particularly with respect to poetry.
In rispetto di poesia, he said. And I said, Yes, in American
We call it "moose" and mentioned several poets,
Frank O'Hara among them, who were quite famous,
As fame goes in our sort of work, for their moose.
He wondered if there were an American expression
To convey the general concept of "Eugenio Montale."
And I said, Yes, we call it "George Seferis." I also observed—
I was showing off, but how often do you get to talk
To Eugenio Montale—that, in my view, the prose of Seferis,
Especially his diaries from the last years of the war
And the slow wakening to that devastation after,
Was even greater than his poems, though his poems
At their best gave off pure light like the light that flares
From the white walls on the cliffs above the harbor in Skios
Which can make the eyes ache. He canted his head
Politely and asked if among Americans the worship
Of the Virgin Mary was a custom. And I said that it was
And that in the cities of the Middle West and probably
The towns, it was especially intense among the mothers
Of children with grave illnesses who heaped flowers
In enormous quantities before her altar and he nodded
And said that this was also the case in the cities of Italy.
And they light candles? he asked. And I said, Yes, candles.

STANZAS FOR A SIERRA MORNING

Looking for wildflowers: scruffy yarrow
With its deep roots for this dry place
And fireweed which likes disturbed ground.

There were lots of them. A bright white yarrow,
And the fireweed was the brilliant magenta
Some women put on their lips for summer evenings.

The water of the creek ran clear over creekstones
And a pair of dove-white plovers fished the rills
A sandbar made in one of the turnings of the creek.

You couldn't have bought the sky's blue.
Not in the silk markets of Samarkand. Not
In any market between Xi'an and Venice.

Which doesn't mean that it doesn't exist.
Isn't that, after all, what a stanza is for,
So that after a night of listening, unwillingly,

To yourself think, you can walk, idly,
Through some morning market, sipping tea,
An eye out for that scrap of immaculate azure.

PATCHES OF SNOW IN JULY

In June there had been weeks of unseasonable cold and several days of snow in the Tahoe Sierra, so that city people were driving up to ski on the Fourth of July. Ten days later, the tips of the pines seemed to be on fire with the neon green of new growth, and along the Truckee River wildflowers had the raw look of early spring, as if they were astonished at themselves for having forced the dead earth. Coming into the valley, something about the way the grasses and wildflowers and trees climbed the mountains right up to treeline, as if they were a young orchestra hitting high notes, and the way the white patches of snow in the saddles of bare rock between the massive peaks glittered in the sun undid me. If that's the right word. Undid. Woke up. Life in its exuberance rushing straight uphill toward death. The night before I had been reading from an anthology of seventeenth-century English poetry.

Death in Infancy

> *Nor let the milky fonts that bathe your thirst*
> *Be your delay;*
> *The place that calls you hence is, at the worst,*
> *Milk all the way.*
>
> —RICHARD CRASHAW

Almost as if one should not speak of it,
who has not, as a parent, had the shock of it.
Too late to tell them that life is a breath,
or that life which is so fair is so unfair.
Too soon to be sure one is not hearing
through a wall the last crying before sleep,
to know a lullaby from inconsolable lament.
Hush now, just begun. Sleep a little. Sleep.

—

Death in Childhood

Which cover lightly, gentle earth!
—BEN JONSON

He was a solemn and delicate little boy.
His father was a physicist, and I could see
on the day that I watched him on the beach
in La Jolla, that the shell in his hand was no toy
to him. He had learned to look at things.
Also to treat information with great seriousness.
So he studied it carefully and explained to me
that the successive ridges on the curvature
were the stages of its growth, and what form
of carbon calcium was, and how evolution
had worked its way up to invertebrates.
He would brush back a shock of blond hair
from his eyes to look up and see if I followed him.
The hole in his heart was not what killed him;
it was the way that his lungs had to labor
because of the defect. The surf was breaking
through irises of light, quick small rainbows
down the beach as far as one could see.
He had to have been a very avid listener.
It seemed to me to mean that he'd been loved,
and wanted to be like his father, which was why
it was so delicious to him to be talking
to almost any adult about all there is to know.

———

Death in Adolescence

We shall new shadows make the other way

—JOHN DONNE

On a Tuesday morning, early, on the lawn by the pond,
there's a scattering still of red and white rose petals
from the Sunday wedding. Slow ripple of wind
on the green pond. Quick rippling in the aspen's leaves.
Is there anything that doesn't stand for them in summer?
Insects skimming the surface tension of the water.
The small circles their legs make on that glass.
The pert, dusky insect-eating bird perched on a chunk
of grey granite—the kind they call glacial errata—
that the reflection on the pond reads back to the sun
as a shade of warm, pale brown, almost an umber.
The young man in my lecture course always took
the same seat, halfway up, until one morning
when he didn't. It was almost the end of the term.
(His parents wrote to ask to see his final essay.
I looked in my tall stack of unread student papers
and I found it—on voices speaking from the dead
in Dickinson.) Is there anything they are figured by?
The thick swarming of insects at the pond's edge
that has made the perching bird so pert—someone
who lived into her thirties and studied entomology
has observed that they swarm that way—the males—
because it's efficient, easier to be noticed en masse
if you were a female looking for a mate, and in this one way
at least it is like high school. The girl who dies
of being fat, of not having breasts, of too-thick calves
or acne. The boy who dies of stuttering, of the distance
between his imagination of himself and how he imagines

he is seen. They are the children with their backpacks
in the morning and a sullen look, as if their parents
had sent them out to peddle damaged goods. The boy
who dies because his roommate films him having sex
with another boy and puts it on the internet, so that
everyone he knows can gather in his mind and giggle
as they watch him come and cry out loud oh! oh! oh!
In what form not pray to their presence still
among us? As salt on the tongue, as used candy wrappers
on the street. White candles in summer, pumpkin-colored
in the fall. Out, out, brief—. The steamed, churning window
in a washing machine. Isn't that them? All
straightaways on highways, all long slow curves
on mountain roads. The red glow fading in the tubes
of old radio sets when you turned them off. The tinny sound
of the recorded voices of disused comedians. "Say, Molly,
why didn't you take the elevator up? Because the sign said,"
and the audience (in 1933? 1938) is already laughing.
New tennis shoes. Old tennis shoes. Arthur Axelrod,
you are the old, tall, Gothic arches that the elms made
down the settled, handsome old neighborhoods in Buffalo
before elm disease took them, and you are the active
youth orchestras of bacteria in the spores of elm disease,
and the huge Morris Louis canvas of color disappearing
in the abstract expressionist galleries at the Albright-Knox.
My first job. The English department was a Quonset hut
and the department was full of poets. There must have been
a dozen poets and a precocious high school boy came
after school to wander in the halls. I used to write
like Creeley, he would say. Basil Bunting got his meter
from Scarlatti, he would say. A pink-faced boy, plump,
as if from a mild deficit in testosterone. I can't seem
to finish my Olson elegy, he said. His classmates
didn't know, people said laughing, what to make

of him. Winter can stand for them, spring, of course.
Even fall in certain turbulent or reluctant or tender
stages of its changing. What doesn't stand for them
is what's old, worn down, used up. Though what's old
and skilled, the skills almost unconsciously absorbed
so that the pleasure of them also is almost unconscious,
may be a place to stand to see them. Not the point of view
of the young actor whose agent calls before the interview
to remind him not to comb his hair. The old actor
who goes off in a tweed hat and bow tie with plaid shirt
in the morning to do the insurance company commercial.
Before his teeth cleaning appointment, before his lunch
with his step-daughter to try again to straighten out
their misunderstanding on the phone, before he arrives
at the theater and does his stretches and takes a lozenge
for his throat, before he begins his makeup that will run
with his sweat some five hours later when he hurls himself
on stage howling "Never, never, never, never, never!"

THOSE WHO DIE IN THEIR TWENTIES

Eyes, hands, and feet they had like mine
—Thomas Traherne

Joe was the first person I knew who cultivated languid boredom
as a mark of superior intelligence, like the characters
I'd read about in English novels. He was handsome, brilliant,
gay, which you knew about him immediately and did not,
normally, know about people immediately in those days.
His grandfather owned factories in Cincinnati, it was said,
and the New Yorkers I was getting to know teased him
for referring to himself in California as an "easterner,"
as if in this one way this person whose style was acid frankness
had fudged his vita to disown the ordinary Middle West.
We told him he was rich. "Trust fund, not rich," he said.
"It means I'll be another assistant professor of classics
with slightly nicer things than everybody else."
The impressive part of which was that, while most of us
were worried about surviving graduate school at all
or whether it was a fit and, if not, what then, Joe had,
already, assumed a success that seemed to him second-rate,
which in those days, oddly enough, like the clothes
he wore so easily, gave him a silvery beauty in our eyes
that the note he left when he killed himself confirmed.
"It's Tuesday and overcast. It seems a thing to do."
In the twenties a friend is a world, and a style of speaking
or dressing, a social class or an ethnicity, a way of walking
or thinking, if it shimmers, is almost erotically attractive,
partly because it's an age when wealth or beauty or brains
or brute force or swinging one's shoulders with a special grace
seems like grace. If you leave the world you grew up in,

which, if it happens, happens to most Americans at that age,
there's something in that eros of the other that gives to the desirer
or admirer another pair of eyes, sophisticates the world
just when our appetite for glamour in its various forms
is sharpest. And so, terrible as it is in a way to say it, the world
we lose when we lose the ones who die in their twenties
—I am not speaking of siblings or lovers—or parents—
doesn't lose the brilliance of its luster. And even death,
because it is terrible, does not taste terrible. Because
the first adult grief makes us feel adult. His body,
when they recovered it, was shipped home. We met
to speak of him at parties and what we said to each other,
mutely, in the silence of the first exchange of looks
was something like—so this is death, the real deal,
and now whatever it is we're in is not just made up
anymore. None of us knew him well enough to know
what hurt him into the Pacific. It seems to me now
that he probably died of being gay in the wrong decade.
Then I thought that his death had a certain glamour,
even though its glamour was despair, which he'd have liked
and probably imagined, and that he shouldn't have.

PLANH OR DIRGE FOR THE ONES WHO DIE
IN THEIR THIRTIES

If life is a day, then thirty-three—
There's a green wind on the pond,
It's summer on the pond—

Is near to an unshadowed noon.
There's a green wind on the pond,
It's summer on the pond.

Frank O'Hara, Charlie Parker,
It's summer on the pond.
There's a green wind on the pond.

Sylvia Plath, Arthur Rimbaud.
There's a green wind on the pond.
It's summer on the pond.

Our dear Peter at thirty-six.
It's summer on the pond.
There's a green wind on the pond.

His wife was pregnant seven months.
It's summer on the pond.
There's a green wind on the pond.

He was running a "half-marathon."
There's a green wind on the pond.
It's summer on the pond.

We threw white roses in the grave.
There's a green wind on the pond.
It's summer on the pond.
It's summer on the pond.

HARVEST: THOSE WHO DIE EARLY IN THE MIDDLE YEARS

As lightning, or a Taper's light

—JOHN DONNE

And now a trick-of-the-senses dissolve:
it's not a Sierra waterfall you're hearing.
It sounds like a waterfall. The peasants of Osaka
are cutting barley in a field. Listen to the rhythm
of it. You can almost feel the muggy heat, the
sour, heady, cut grass odor in the air.
The clapping sound is the crew boss
keeping time. Jane Kenyon, cancer at forty-seven.
Larry Levis, heart at forty-nine. Ray Carver
who had met Tess and beat alcohol which
was going to kill him, cancer at fifty.
Bill Matthews who liked looking ravaged,
heart at fifty-five. He was dressing for the opera.
All of them suddenly become the work
they managed to get done. The man walking
past the field in Osaka is Yosa Buson who is thinking
of his dead master, Bashō, thinking of his childhood
in Osaka where the farmers planted barley
first. It was the early summer crop. And it is
like thirst or hunger, the feeling that the grassy
sweetness of the piled up stalks of barley
stirs in him when a sick man passes
carried in a litter, so that, thinking of his master,
dead a hundred years, who taught him simplicity
and suggestion and exactness in an art,
and who died at fifty, he thought
to write: *A sick man passing*—five syllables—

in a palanquin; *summer*—seven syllables—
And a violent enjambment for Japanese verse—
is the autumn of barley. Ronald Blythe, the Englishman
interned by the Japanese in the World War,
amused himself by translating old poems
and made a version of Bashō's death poem—
Sick on a journey my dreams wander
the withered fields—and of Buson's poem
and I like to think he had been reading Walt Whitman
and had come to the moment in "Song of Myself"
when Whitman, describing the cascade of passersby
on Broadway, notices *the flap of the curtain'd litter—*
sick man inside, borne to the hospital and
later in the poem where the context is war,
the ambulanza slowly passing trailing
its red drip and also, because he was English
and had found a copy of the poems in the library
of the abandoned embassy, read or recalled
because he already had them, as we say, by heart,
those lines of Tennyson that came to the poet
as a verbal music when he was out walking
in Derbyshire: It was *only,* he wrote, *reapers,*
reaping early in among the bearded barley.

SECOND PERSON

That summer, after your friend had shot herself the previous November
    in her backyard garden—it was the morning after Thanksgiving——

And after the sudden death from cancer of another friend, a prose writer—
who had been living in Italy with his fourth wife

And seemed after a long struggle to be working suddenly at the top of
    his form, you had left off writing a tribute to be read at the memorial
    service

For the one friend in order to go to the hospital to visit the other, who, it
    was clear (his family gathered around him.

His wife, children from two marriages) cancer was finishing off,

A fact which he seemed to regard with bitter clarity, even contempt.

He'd had a gift for expecting the worst, and here was the thing itself.
    He was leaving behind a beautiful woman and an unfinished book

And—they had been living in Italy—the silver green of wheat fields in
    the Umbrian dusk. He had liked coffee,

Fussed over its preparation, loved the high gloss of the leather on Italian
    shoes.

You did get your brief memorial talk written, and delivered it, mourning
    in a room full of mourners, mostly her friends,

Mostly people in middle age and late middle age and so getting newly accustomed to the frequency of memorial services,

And yourself new also to this experience—not of death—but of a subtle, though not that day that subtle, acceleration in the occasions for mourning,

You felt death there in the wood-paneled room with its elegant, coffered ceiling, its busts of authors and composers, its bookshelves where,

You saw suddenly, the dead were sleeping like the princess in the fairy tale, and could be awakened and set speaking by the caress of attention,

Felt death, that is, to be a somber and dignified presence, a figure of some authority, not a funeral director exactly,

More like the respected principal of an honorable but famously formal school, or even a valet, a gentleman's gentleman

Who was older than you and wiser and understood all the forms of the world's etiquettes and had acquired the habit of waiting patiently

While people experienced themselves, and afterwards your own life continued according to its various contingencies

And you found yourself in Paris in the Odéon neighborhood on a little street near the medical school with its loud, late cafés and bars

For the students and interns getting off work at the hospital, so you did not sleep well but woke anyway to fulfill the promise you had made

To finish a translation of Pablo Neruda's "Barcarole" and "Sólo la Muerte," the poem in which, in the last lines, death is an admiral standing on a hill in the harbor mouth

Reviewing his fleet. And this is why you needed the second person
singular, to describe the mornings walking up Rue des Quatre-Vents
to the Café Mairie

On the wetted-down cobbles of the summer street, looking in shop
windows as you went, death in the etchings of old boats and in the rich
rotogravures

Of tropical flowers, to your coffee and the view onto Saint-Sulpice, and, a
line at a time, Neruda's poem. You could have said, "That summer

After my friend had shot herself" or "That summer after his friend
had shot herself," but it was you who walked the streets those
mornings,

Wavering a bit among the grammatical propositions as you woke to the
early summer coolness in the air,

You studying the piles of fruit in the little markets and the gilded Empire
sewing chairs in the antique shops,

You lingering over the shop specializing in anthropological texts with its
sheets, torn probably from the books, to be sold separately, of cannibals
from Borneo

And high-necked, barebreasted Nubian queens, because you had the
strong sense that death was tending it all,

The little pears wrapped in paper on the espaliered trees in the
Luxembourg Gardens, the house you passed sometimes on Rue
Fleury

Where Gertrude Stein had spent her days writing sentences like "Tea
towels aren't necessarily,"

Past the small hotel across the square from Saint-Sulpice where Stein put
   up Thornton Wilder when he visited and where, now,

The young woman brought her green wooden wagon piled high with
   white and blue irises to sell separately or in bunches—

What is it about irises that makes you want to describe a sheaf of them
   as "lithe," as if they were longlegged young women bathing together

After a round of golf or tennis? You were in that sort of neighborhood,
   and wondered briefly how the day

Might have been different, been colored differently, were the woman at
   the wagon old and Moroccan with dark brown, well-worn hands

And not a Sorbonne graduate in pigtails and a jaunty longshoreman's cap,
   moving like a dancer as she unloaded and heaped up her flowers,

And you did not have a Spanish dictionary, so after you had done a
   morning's work, had written in long hand

Next to the Spanish text, "its incessant red waters would come to flood,
   and it would ring out with shadows, ring out like death,"

You would gather up your books and walk back down Rue Valmont to
   Quatre-Vents and then to Rue Princesse and the Village Voice Bookshop

Where you knew Odile and Michael would not mind if you went upstairs
   into the alcove of foreign language dictionaries

To look up the word you'd translated or guessed at translating with your
   sketchy Spanish as "incessant." You did this for weeks,

And began, as you walked, to notice the young men from the suburbs,
   Martiniquan or Senegalese, or Arabic, perhaps Algerian or Tunisian,

And the young Vietnamese, sweeping the street in front of the restaurants
   that catered to the well-off folk of the arrondissement and to visitors
   like you,

Specializing in the cuisines of the French countryside, the home cooking
   of Gascony and Alsace and the Languedoc,

That the children of the proprietors didn't want to cook anymore, and you
   thought of the young black men in your country,

Shot by police in a train station after a scuffle, or shot coming home from
   a late trip to an all-night convenience store

And you wondered about the mothers in the Parisian suburbs, in what
   uniforms or regalia death appeared to them when their sons went out
   into the night,

And felt mildly sick, thinking about the courtesies of death and the
   sense of propriety or the predatory lunge with which it distributed its
   presence in the world, social class

By social class, war zone by war zone, brutal here, gentle there, as if you
   were being wakened again by and to an unfairness

As labyrinthine as the city itself, whose districts, whose boulevards and
   alleys, gardens and arcades, you wandered in the afternoons

And so you came more and more to look forward to the quiet mornings
   with the poems,

Looking up different words each day, taking Neruda a line at a time—
   "With a sound like dreams or branches or the rain,"

"and the great wings of the sea would wheel round you." By the middle of
   July it was hot and you walked long hours in the city

And by eight o'clock—you had begun living in time—when you came
   back to the neighborhood of Saint-Germain-des-Prés,

And you would sit at one of the outdoor tables and the proprietor would
   set down in front of you, with a delicate glassy sound,

A chilled glass of Lillet, you would remind yourself that the proprietor
   was not death,

Nor was the Lillet, nor the handsome couple at the next table ordering
   grilled river fish.

THREE OLD MEN

1.

Midnight! To bed!
Something will come to you in the morning.
It will be a Monday in summer, a beginning.
There'll be misty sun in the morning, wind in the trees.
Monday is a subject. Visit it
In the morning.

2.

Saint Monday, the old gardener in Shelford
Called it. Mr. Acker. "Why *Saint* Monday?"
I had asked. "Because it takes care of you,
Doesn't it? If you've had a bit on Sunday,
You start off at a nice slow pace."

That voice, coming to me
Across forty years. My daughter,
Who became a scholar of memory,
Used to like to talk to him
About the names of plants. "Sheep's parsley,"
He'd say. "Grows like billy-o.
I've been hoeing it out all my life
And now they want me to grow it.
They think it looks rural."

3.

And I remembered the old poet's voice
When I was forty or so and in agony.
He must have been seventy. He it was
Who shrugged and said, "You can't kill delight
In the people you love, or in yourself."
Who said "So you hurt others,
And are hurt." Paused, looked amused. "And, of course,
The more you loved and had been loved,
The worse you're apt to hurt or be hurt.
You know the expression 'in for a penny,
In for a pound'?" Found that scrap in my notebooks
And thought to make a Monday poem from it.

Moon's day. He was a poet
Of the grandeur of wounds.
"My mother's breast was thorny
And father I had none," he had written.
And "The night nailed like an orange
to my brow." He lived to be a hundred
And, visiting him the day after his birthday,
I said, "Stanley, you're a hundred!"
And he said, "I don't recommend it,"
Who had watched his wife die,
Raving with dementia
In the hospital room they had made from the dining room
Where he had served us, eyes wide with self-delight,
His own bouillabaisse from a steaming tureen
On a festive fall night thirty years before.

4.

People do not stroll in Manhattan in January.
Coming out of Stanley's, I looked at the bodies
On Fifth Avenue bundled against the cold,
Leaning into the wind and going about their furious purposes
And I thought of people I've hurt with my hunger
And thought, "Delight?" I knew that for Stanley
It was William Blake's word, had to do with some pact
He'd made with himself as a young man to live his life.

5.

My daughter, at my grandson's graduation—
We were standing in a garden
In the muggy Midwestern heat of a late afternoon
In June, drinking a cocktail called Dark and Stormy
And studying the handsome young celebrants hugging each other—
They'd been out drinking and carousing the night before
So this Saturday was a sort of Saint Monday
And my daughter said, "Pop, you remember that old gardener
In the village in England, what was his name?"
And I smiled and said, "Mr. Acker,"
And she smiled and said, "Yes, that's right.
Mr. Acker."

6.

Every day a moon, every day a match struck
And flaring. "Talent is one thing,"
Stanley said when I was thirty or so.
As if he thought I might get a little high

From having a first book published.
"You need character for the long haul.
Nobody wants you to be a poet."

7.

Died at almost a hundred and one.
"My mother's breast was thorny."
He had made a life.
His ashes in the garden he made
Of the salt air on the Cape.

8.

It's Tuesday's child must work for a living.
Tyr's day. The god of war, god
Of one-handed combat. Full of grace
Or not. Tomorrow I'm
Going to hike to the waterfall
And listen to the sound of it.

PABLO NERUDA: ONLY DEATH

There are isolated cemeteries,
Tombs filled with mute bones,
The heart going through a tunnel,
Shadowy, shadowy, shadowy:
We die as if a ship were going down inside us,
Like a drowning in the heart,
Like falling endlessly from the skin to the soul.

There are corpses,
There are feet of clammy stone,
There is death in the bones,
Like pure sound,
Like a bark without a dog,
Growing out of certain bells, certain tombs,
Swelling in the humidity like a lament or like rain.

Alone, sometimes, I see
Coffins under sail
Weighing anchor with the pale dead, with women in their dead braids,
With bakers white as angels,
Thoughtful girls married to accountants,
Coffins climbing the vertical river of the dead,
The bruise-colored river,
Laboring upstream, sails billowing with the sound of death,
Billowing with the sound of the silence of death.

It's sound that death is drawn to,
Like a shoe without a foot, like a suit with no man in it,
It's drawn to knock with a ring, stoneless and fingerless,
It's drawn to call out without a mouth, a tongue, a throat.

No question, you can hear death's footsteps,
And death's clothes rustle, quiet as a tree.

I don't know, I don't get it, I can hardly see
But I believe that death's song is the color of wet violets,
Violets accustomed to the earth,
Because the face of death is green,
And the gaze of death is green
With the sharp wetness of the leaf of a violet
And its serious color of wintry impatience.

But death also goes about the earth riding a broom,
Licking the ground looking for the dead ones;
Death is in the broom,
It's death's tongue looking for the dead,
It's death's needle that needs threading.

Death is in the bedsteads:
In the slow mattresses, in the black blankets
Death stretches out like a clothesline, and then suddenly blows,
Blows a dark sound that swells the sheets
And beds are sailing into a harbor
Where death is waiting, dressed as an admiral.

TO BE ACCOMPANIED BY FLUTE AND ZITHER

We live on a coastal hill with a view west onto a bay, a mountain, a rust-gold bridge, and the sea beyond them. There are several sleeping islands on the bay, dark with chaparral,

And east of us in summer gold hills of wild grasses with a scattering of oaks on the hillsides a green so dark they are almost blue, and with madrone and laurel in the canyons,

And east of those trees a wide valley, hot and flat, the remnant bed of torrential glacial rivers, once an immense lake, and then a bog and then a meadow so thick with wildflowers in the late spring you could hear the bee-hum before you crested the Coast Range hills to look down on it, colors so thick and variegated that they seemed to be breathing,

Breathing, O Elysium, and now farm country mostly, industrial farming, with a strong smell of onion fields in summer, and river towns along the sloughs, and an endless rosary of shopping malls built to collapse in a generation or so, with parking lots full of empty cars and car windshields glittering in the midday heat,

And east of the valley the slow rise of red earth foothills, oakwood giving way to pine, and then a gradual climb seven thousand feet to the mountain massif of glacier-carved granite, mountain lakes blue-green with snow melt, and lodgepole pine, Jeffrey pine, sugar pine, incense cedar forests that smell of pine sap and pineapple and the scintillant high mountain air and, even in summer, snow patches in the saddles between peaks,

And among the cols and tarns of the mountain escarpment, there are immense lakes turquoise blue to the depths, with emerald green at the deeper shorelines, and small lakes, ice-blue in the afternoon when the sky clouds up, and small meadow valleys that must once have been lakes, long ago, where small streams splash down a canyon, some small Squaw Creek to water a meadow, a ski resort now, a bit lazy and full of tourists in shorts in the summer,

But there are paths out of that valley under the pines, the loud jays of the mountains squawking and squawking, and scarlet gilia with their little trumpet flowers and the dangling intricate red and gold flower of the columbine, and red also for Indian paintbrush,

Because the mountain is kind to hummingbirds, which can see red as the bees can't, and for the bees the brilliant blue of the larkspur and the fuzzy soiled white of pearly everlasting, and for everyone the bright yellow monkey flower that likes the spray of plunging water,

It breathes well there, breathes, my dear, and that may be you standing in the trail above it under the sheered granite, you among buckbrush and huckleberry oak with the field guide in hand naming the lichens—

Have you noticed that this is an anniversary poem? a medicine bundle for the hard stretches when we carry what we've glimpsed into the grinding days down the trail there which we'll be walking, muscles a little sore, as a breeze comes up and gives its lightness to the summer air.

ABBOTT'S LAGOON: OCTOBER

The first thing that is apt to raise your eyes
Above the dove-grey and silvery thickets
Of lupine and coyote bush and artichoke thistle
On the sandy, winding path from the parking lot
To the beach at Abbott's Lagoon is the white flash
Of the marsh hawk's rump as it skims low
Over the coastal scrub. White-crowned sparrows,
Loud in the lupine even in October, even
In the drizzly rain, startle and disappear.
The bush rabbits freeze, then bolt and disappear,
And the burbling songs and clucks of the quail
That you may not even have noticed you were noticing
Go mute and you are there in October and the rain,
And the hawk soars past, first hawk, then shadow
Of a hawk, not much shadow in the rain, low sun
Silvering through clouds a little to the west.
It's almost sundown. And this is the new weather
At the beginning of the middle of the California fall
When a rain puts an end to the long sweet days
Of our September when the skies are clear, days mild,
And the roots of the plants have gripped down
Into the five- or six-month drought, have licked
All the moisture they are going to lick
From the summer fogs, and it is very good to be walking
Because you can almost hear the earth sigh
As it sucks up the rain, here where mid-October
Is the beginning of winter which is the beginning
Of a spring greening, as if the sound you are hearing
Is spring and winter lying down in one another's arms

Under the hawk's shadow among the coastal scrub,
Ocean in the distance and the faintest sound of surf
And a few egrets, bright white, working the reeds
At the water's edge in October in the rain.

CHRISTMAS IN AUGUST

for Dan Halpern

Towns on the Northern California coast are foggy in August
With shafts of startled sunlight sometimes in the afternoon.
It's hard to say what season you are in, so, in the market
This morning, idling past the sacks of corn flour with my cart,
A snatch of the lilt of Spanish came into my head.
Maria C. makes a hundred tamales every year
For Christmas Eve and likes to talk, when I see her
In town on a cold December day, about her schedule:
The day she roasts the pork and boils the chicken, the day
She spends simmering the mole—onions and garlic, of course,
Bay leaves and chiles, guajillo or chipotle for smokiness,
And oregano—"How much?" you ask Maria and she shrugs,
"Un poquito,"—and at this season, sticks of cinnamon,
A little ground pumpkin seed, cumin, some chocolate—
Her sister likes green olives—you simmer it for hours
While you knead the masa with pork fat from the roast
And the seasoned water you boiled the chicken in—
And then Christmas Eve eve, when the children help you
Fashion the tamales in their *hojas*. That was the phrase
I remembered in the market, the one about the young girls
And their *manos rápidos*. It made me think of Christmas
In the Berkeley hills and the old man's hands—a refugee
Professor from another generation, he would seem chagrined
When I saw him in the market, as if we had been caught
In some unmanly compromise when we should be home
Writing treatises on medieval Polish grammarians.
But he loved preparing herring on Christmas Eve
And I can visualize his old hands, not so quick,

Slicing pieces of the fatty Baltic fish, assembling
Juniper berries, the vinegar and peppercorns and olive oil,
Bay leaves and cloves. There is, I'm sure, some Polish phrase
For the right amount of mustard, meaning "just enough."
At our house we peel chestnuts on Christmas Eve morning,
My beloved in her apron browning onions and celery
For the stuffing, her flowered apron all business,
As if she were commandeering the ship of the world,
Which in a way, on that day, she does. Outside
It was August, the planet just turning toward the dark,
A long way and not a long way from the short, dark days
We gather to celebrate the light surviving through.

AN ARGUMENT ABOUT POETICS IMAGINED AT SQUAW VALLEY
AFTER A NIGHT WALK UNDER THE MOUNTAIN

My friend Czesław Miłosz disapproved of surrealism.
Not hard to construct, in imagination, the reasons why.
Late night and late winter in Warsaw: two friends
Are stopped by the police of the General Government
Who speak atrocious Polish. Because of their leather jackets—
Where would two young Poles get new brown leather jackets
In the winter of 1943?—either they were black marketeers,
The cops reasoned, or special enough to be left alone.
The older cop who had been a policeman in Berlin
In the quiet precincts of Charlottenburg where he had learned
To go along and get along and who wanted now
Only to do his job well enough to avoid being sent
To the Russian front, where he'll either be blown up
Or lose his toes to frostbite, wants nothing of this pinch.
He's the one who lets the poet slip away.
The other, younger, a machinist in Cologne before the war,
Is more ambitious. He asks the second man what he does.
Which for the young Pole is a quandary. Does he say
He is a philosopher, which is what he thinks of as his profession,
Or a teamster, which is how he makes his living now
To avoid collaborating with the Germans? And secondly
Should he answer him in Polish or in his perfect German?
He is completing, after work, in his drafty garret room
A treatise on the Apollonian and Dionysiac personalities
Described by Friedrich Nietzsche from a partly Marxist,
Partly kabbalistic perspective. He feels instinctively
That the danger lies in claiming a superior social status
And so he says in Polish that he is a teamster, and the cop
Thinks—aha! black market—and takes him in.

He's interrogated, turned over to the SS, beaten,
Interrogated some more, identified as a communist
And an intellectual and sent east to Auschwitz
Where he eventually dies, shot, some of the stories say,
Wasted by typhus and diarrhea, say the others.
The poet hears one of these versions of the news
On the same spring day that he is contemplating
A large, polished porcelain giraffe bobbing up and down
To the strains of the Vienna Waltz on a holiday carousel
While gunfire crackles on the other side of the ghetto wall.
Warsaw had been a Russian garrison town for a century.
Now it's a German garrison town and the pretty Polish girl
On the giraffe is licking a pink cloud of cotton candy
And flirting with the German officer on the zebra,
Which is also bobbing up and down, and the sheen
On his high black boots, the poet notices involuntarily,
Has picked up the reflection of the sun in the small pools
Of spring rain on the warped tarmac apron of the carousel.
After that he doesn't want to read about French poets
Walking lobsters on a leash and doesn't want to seem
To celebrate the fact that the world makes no sense.
This is how, anyway, I imagine the state of mind
Produced by the fragments of the stories he would tell me.
And here inference and anecdote give way to argument.
I would quote André Breton to him in the English translation.
My wife with the armpits of nettletrap and St. John's Eve.
And he would say, or, anyway, now, in my imagination,
He would say, "Well, yes, of course, I assent to armpits.
And metaphors, at which Breton excelled, just as Modigliani
Excelled at armpits. Who does not love metaphor? Its quickness
That gives us the world to taste with our common senses.
I'll tell you what terrifies me: it is the idea that 'this is like that
Is like this is like that' could be all of the story, endlessly
Repeated, the poor human imagination having evolved this

Brilliant swiftness of perception and then been stuck there,
Like a hamster in a cage, groping in the endless turnstiles
Of resemblance. We are to celebrate this? As a final conquest
Of absurdity by absurdity? The armpits of those women in Modigliani,
On the contrary, are the hollows of their arms—like this, perhaps,
Or like that, but finally this woman exposing to us this tender nest
Or dark sweetness of a wet-duck's-feather tuft of hair
In a gesture, notice, that lifts the breast slightly, indolently,
And lifts the rosy nipple and offers it to us, one of the gifts—
Also sunrise, the scent of linen, of the air before first snow—
That the world has to give poor mortals among the terrors
And confusions of being what we are." "Well,"
I might have said, "if you permit me to get technical,
Modigliani is making a generalized representation
Of the idea of a particular woman." And he: "Exactly.
A particular being. General because being this and not that,
This not like that, this one mortal thing, is what mortality
Has given us in common." "And that is the Miłoszian religion?"
"Yes," he laughs. "In my religion, if we are going to starve,
We will starve on the pears of Cézanne and the apples of Chardin."
He squints a little. "In my religion metaphor makes us ache
Because things are, and are what they are, and perish.
Let us not neglect to consider the slow withering
Of the pale skin of that girl and her nest of lymph nodes
And the pheromones of love and fear. And we mustn't fail
To mention lymphatic cancers, nature's brutally stupid way
Of clearing the earth for organisms freed, temporarily,
From withering and disease and the misfiring of that avidity
To reproduce which is the special trick of the cells we were made of
In some chemical slime. And, on the subject of armpits, let us not
Neglect the distinctive smell of fear, which reminds us
That in Mr. Darwin's horrific scheme we are to find beautiful
The fact that, among the higher mammals, the sauce
That gives spice to their meat is the adrenaline of pure terror,

Or worse, the adrenaline of the chase and then of terror,
And, for all we know, of despair, in the prey they are devouring.
Nature is, after all, chemistry and chemistry is this
Becomes that becomes this becomes that endlessly
Through endless witherings, endless contortions
Of mammal and reptile and insect suffering and fear.
What does it know of this armpit? That breast? Those lips
Turned to the mirror for a glistening and reddening
And the way she, a girl who did not feel pretty as a girl,
Examines her plucked, arched, perfectly elegant eyebrow
And pats lightly the slick set of her hair, a 1910s set,
That decade's set, no other's, of her thick auburn hair?"
"Do you know who she was?" I asked, suddenly curious.
"Well there were two women. Jeanne Hébuterne
Who killed herself—threw herself out a window—
She was pregnant with his child—the year after he died.
She was French. Our odalisque of the raised arms
Was Lunia Czechowska. Modigliani's dealer Zborowski
Was a poet, a minor one, and he introduced Lunia
To the painter. Zborowski was a friend of my uncle.
But he died the year I arrived in Paris that first time,
So I never met him, though I did meet Czechowska."
"You met Czechowska?" "She had me to tea.
I was twenty-one. She must have been about forty.
Thick in the waist, and looked it. It was winter
And she wore tweed. She tested me by conducting
Our interviews—mostly about my uncle's poetry
And Zborowski's—entirely in French. I remember
Thinking that her hands looked old, early arthritis
Perhaps, and were somehow beautiful, something
Delicate in the way she served the little Noël cakes
And the tea, which I devoured. I was living
On my student's stipend and then felt humiliated
That I'd cleared the plate before she'd touched it."

He laughed. "And I remember her scent. Amaryllis.
The apartment near the bookstore on Rue Dupuytren
Smelled of the ginger in the cakes and black tea
And her scent of amaryllis like dry summer grass."
Czesław was buried in a crypt—in the Krakovian church
Of St. Peter of the Rock—among other Polish notables.
I hated the idea of it and still do, that his particular body
Is lying there in a cellar of cold marble and old bones
Under the weight of two thousand years of the Catholic Church.
(Thinking about this still years later, imagining this dialogue
In the Sierra dark under the shadowy mass of the mountain
And the glittering stars.) Not liking the fact that it is,
Perhaps, what he would have wanted. "You should
Have been buried"—I'm still talking to him—"on a grassy hillside
Open to the sun (the Lithuanian sun the peasants
Carved on crosses in the churchyard in your childhood)
And what you called in one poem 'the frail lights of birches.'"
And he might have said no. He might have said,
"I choose marble and the Catholic Church because
They say no, to natural beauty that lures us and kills us.
I say no until poor Modigliani and Zborowski
And Czechowska, the girl of the raised arms and breast,
And the grown woman with her ginger cakes
And already liver-spotted hands, and Jeanne Hébuterne
And her unborn child, have risen from the dead."
And I say, There are other ways of thinking about this.
You described headlights sweeping a field
On a summer night, do you remember? I can quote to you
The lines. You said you could sense the heartbeat
Of the living and the dead. It was a night in July, he said,
In Pennsylvania—to me then an almost inconceivably romantic name—
And the air was humid and smelled of wet earth after rain.
I remember the night very well. Those lines not so much.

CYMBELINE

Everything we do is explaining the sunrise.
Dying explains it. Making love explains it.

The last plays of Shakespeare explain it.
We're just as ignorant as at the beginning.

We make Stonehenge over and over
Thinking it will do some good to know where

Or at least when: flame fissuring up between two stones.
It lifts us as sex arches the body, up, it carries us, up and over,

And no one knows why or when it will stop,
So everything we do is explaining the sunrise.

THE ARCHAEOLOGY OF PLENTY

All you have to do is say some words.
All you have to do is what the birds
Outside your window are doing in the first light
Of a morning in the middle of July. Like you
They have an eye to open. (All you have to do
Is rhyme.) Like you they've slept. (All you have to do
Is live in time.) What leaps, what leapt
To mind is the oddness of "July"
And "sleeps," as in the sentence *Every*
creature sleeps. Who wound (not "eu" but "ow")
A world in which, because the spinning motion
Of a rock in space in relation to a burning storm
Of gasses, causes every organic thing, passing
between hours of light and hours of dark,
(All you have to do is make words sing) to shut down
In the interests of efficiency, so as not to wear out
So soon (All you have to do is make a ring
Of words, a pleasing thing from words)? "Who," of course,
Is a figure of speech. (All you have to do
Is reach into your heavy waking,
The metaphysical nausea that being in your life,
With its bearing and its strifes, its stiffs,
Its stuff, seems to have produced in you,
Reduced you to, and make something with a pleasing,
Or teasing, ring to it; if you can't get rid of it,
Sing to it is all you have to do.)

Dear A———. Driving into these mountains, I had to remind myself that
they are not sacred beings or the visible emanations of some enormous
unseen dower (unless I said they were, if you know what I mean), but
bare rock eroding in the sun. Which led me to think that "rock" was an

inexplicable invention. Which led me to remind myself that "invention" was, in this case, a figure of speech. I think of being afflicted by the pointlessness of the world as described to us by the physical sciences as a late nineteenth-century disease and it seems redundant to be having a bout of it in the early twenty-first century—to have to conjure up my ill-digested understanding of the big bang, to remind myself that while people in shorts in all the malls we pass are eating strawberry ice cream or trying out sleeping postures in the showrooms of mattress discounters or smashing each other with tire irons in fits of road rage, the earth is a fleck of the aftermath of an explosion that eventually took the form of "rock" and is being hurled away, spinning, from its explosive origin and, in the meanwhile, playing out these various organic forms it has evolved, including the convolute matter that is, in me, forming these words. I imagine you are watching your girls running through the sprinkler just now and that's what you should be doing on a summer day. You and D— can have the meaninglessness of the universe, after you've grilled the chicken and eaten the chilled melon balls you let the girls scoop out this afternoon with the melon-ball-fashioning tool and after they've bathed and been storied and you've watched their small mouths make small, even breaths as they fall asleep, by putting some film noir into the DVD player and watching a mostly forgotten actor in one of those really flash suits with the wide lapels and wide, short ties, go down to death for no good reason except that he was—it's the language the French critics loved—a sucker for some dame. I like thinking of you both, my dears. I like thinking of the final sped-up whir and click of the DVD player shutting off and the last picking up of glasses from the coffee table and kids' toys from the farther reaches of the rug, back there, on a summer night, with some large, improbable, named, familiar entity like the Hudson River just outside your window and flowing past you as you fall asleep. It calms me down a little to think of it. Something about the cool sheets just after the music comes up at the end composed by some Russian émigré making very good money and still telling himself that he's going to give it all up and compose sonatas again some day. You, of course, have the kids and the morning to think about. I remembered that as I was

thinking about, or not thinking about, roadkill—one deer, one raccoon,
two skunks, a fox—I think it was a fox, it might have been a coyote,
I drove by fast—a couple of possums, and at least one snake, a garter
snake, I assume, I thought I caught a glimpse of red, though it might have
been blood. The usual carnage as this enormous force of cars ascended
toward pleasure and the pine scent came up and the snow gleamed in
the saddles between crests at Donner Pass, so that the fact of the sun
rising every day seemed less merciless, when I thought about you two
drifting off to sleep after the movie, hovering then between that romantic
imagination of fatality and the practical immanence that will get you up in
the morning.

All you have to do is say the words. You have very little idea
What the birds think they are doing. Or what "think they are doing"
Means inside a bird. All you have to do is say the words
For some imagined others in a world of words, a lull of world
And words that makes a world, or makes a seeing in the dark
As sheet lightning does, sometimes, at night, in summer fields.
Or—I was about to write—like rain just beginning, like hearing
On waking, in the leaves, the sound of rain. Too painful a way,
Or pretty, to make a saying or a singing of all you have to do.

POEM NOT AN ELEGY IN A SEASON OF ELEGIES

They built shallow ponds in the wetlands
All along the Mediterranean shore to rot fish in
And make a condiment. It has a name
Which escapes me. Two thousand years after,
There was a trail through the checkerboard
Of levees made by the dikes, star thistle
And artichoke thistle edging them.
In southern Portugal one summer,
I jogged early, before the onset of the God's anvil
Of the heat of mid-July. Beach in the distance.
Where the Romans must have hauled their triremes up.
There was a slight breeze off the sea
And down the shore a flock of flamingos
Browsing the marsh, and in a pine
Above the golf course a nesting stork.
Galway was alive then, and I think
Oakley was alive then, Jimmye Hillman
Was alive then and the occasion
For my being there saying to myself
And to Tomaž Šalamun who was alive
Then, and probably in Ljubljana (but there were occasions
When I spoke to him despite his absence
And our only casual acquaintance,
And this was one of them). Tomaž owned a boat once
In Dubrovnik, was partners in a boat which,
I had the impression, they leased to smugglers
Who brought in costume jewelry
From department stores in Italy to avoid customs
Which they peddled in the morning market
In the square in Ljubljana or sold to the women's accessories buyer
For the department stores who got a piece of the markup.

This to be taken with a grain of salt or a dollop
Of fermented fish sauce—garum! was the name—
Since I didn't hear this story from Tomaž and was
More or less drunk when I heard it from someone else,
Part of the Šalamunian legend. Tomaž, I said,
Weaving my way among the salt ponds,
I am weaving my way among salt ponds outside Faro,
Ancient Roman salt ponds still almost intact.
There are guys harvesting clams just down the shore
And a flock of blush-colored intertidal birds
Not even a technicolor Giacometti could have invented
And there is a *stork* nesting in a tree on the golf course.
I have no idea what storks mean to Europeans.
In some of the picture books of my childhood
They built nests in chimneys, which gave the villages
A sleepy, peaceful feeling. Since we're the same age,
You must also have sucked your thumb
And studied pictures of storks dozing in twiggy nests
In a Europe where not much of anything happened
As your mother turned the pages. That's what I would say.
Sitting nests, these creatures, for fifty million years.
Tomaž, I remember your saying that, in your opinion,
All bakers should be taught to sing. "It stands to reason,"
I think you said, and I was impressed that you had mastered
That English idiom. Of course, we stand to reason
And lie down to dream. It would have made dough rise.
Tomaž, they should have lit fires in little paper boats
In the harbor at Dubrovnik when you died. When Galway died,
The earth should have groaned, it should have loosed
Lions in the civil streets. When Mark Strand died,
The stars should have traded small ironic witticisms
In a language wholly unintelligible to us but glittering.
For Oakley we should have decommissioned every dam
On the Colorado and floated a sleek white kayak

Through all its turnings from above Glen Canyon
To the Gulf, trailing after it the long self-erasing
Sentence of a silver wake. And thrown a party
Somewhere on the Baja shore. No metaphors yet
For my father-in-law. He still in my head belongs to being.
A vigorous, generous man, hungry for life at ninety-three,
That summer in Faro he was showing his children
A world he'd come to love. He was a farm boy
From the pine woods of southeast Mississippi
And came to be a man who'd loved the world.
He loved speaking the Portuguese he'd acquired
To court his wife, loved walking his sons
And daughter through the ramparts of the old fortresses
And mosques of the Algarve. He was a little amused
By our interest in cuisines, having grown up
On grits and red-eye gravy because that was what there was
On a Depression farm in Mississippi in 1933,
And because one of his earliest memories was the odor
Of his father and brother rinsing excrements from the guts
Of a slaughtered pig. He was, as an old man, mad about writing
And he'd written about that smell and the squealing and the blood.
But he knew the restaurant in Faro where branzino
Was roasted whole and stuffed with rice and raisins.
And something they did with lemon, cinnamon, and garlic.
He's dead now three weeks. By the time we left the table,
He knew the names of the four children of the waitress
And their ages. This was after he had ordered coffee for us
And the beautiful green pears the Arabs fourteen hundred years ago
Had brought from Damascus to plant in al-Andalus.

THE POET AT NINE

Most gods begin with a soft tearing
In the mind, but some begin in the body.
He's found a place to hide so perfect
That he has to struggle not to laugh
And give himself away. It's the time
When children are called in, it's cold.
He shivers, crouching. A few stars.
He listens to the crickets in the dusk.
Possibly it's blood ringing in his ears.

A PERSON SHOULD

The novel is a mirror in the roadway, I saw scrawled
on a blackboard in an empty classroom at a small college
in the Middle West. A Friday in the fall, day's end,
the swift dark descending, the students gone to their parties,
the long blackboards given over to the melancholy
of chalk dust. Underneath the Stendhal in another hand
someone had written very firmly: *Poetry is sheet lightning
in a summer field.* Which I took to mean that a person should
be able to name their psychic condition or make a figure of it
or see it illuminated out there somewhere in the gravid air.
I quoted the lines once to a friend whose husband was ill
with pancreatic cancer, not apropos of what she was enduring,
but because she'd asked me what I was thinking about.
She gave me a long, neutral look as if she were trying
to pick up my tone toward the lines, the two orders
of knowledge they implied. Or perhaps to see—
she was a molecular chemist—if this was some kind
of intellectual parlor game people like me engaged in.
She was a severe person, and literal, and she was suffering—
and too polite or too accustomed to tolerating the peculiarities
of other people, so she just raised an eyebrow and shrugged.
Later, in another hospital corridor, this having to do with the illness
of a sister-in-law from whom she'd been estranged, and with whom,
in the way of some families, she'd gone through the minimally
necessary motions for years in a state of mild mutual antipathy.
On this day, her husband already dead, she sat slightly hunched
and clutched her purse, as if it were a meaningless possession
but a possession, and when she noticed that I was, I suppose,
studying her face, she said by way of explanation,
"I don't know what a good life is." I looked at her hands
gripping the purse and started counting the things

that were keeping me from being spun off the earth
by sheer centripetal motion: my shoes, the name
on my driver's license. I think my concern for her that day
was not one of them. We were not close. I happened to be nearby;
it seemed she shouldn't have to be alone. There were two daughters,
who had gone to school with my children. One was
in New Zealand where I think she taught art history,
one in Belgium and to do with public health. Beautiful women,
or they were as children, and immensely lively,
and I had the impression that they had loved their father
and found their mother intellectual and cold. It seemed
something between insipid and intrusive to ask her
what she was feeling, so, as awkwardly as you can imagine,
I put my arm around her, tentatively, there on the bench
in the hospital corridor. She was not a person whom you hugged
and she ignored my arm and continued to stare at the floor
and said, "It's not enough not to be stupid, not to be
trouble to others." I said, "You and Rachmael survived
so much and you made a life." She glanced at me again
with that neutral, interrogating look and said, "A life."
When I find myself wanting to tell people about the lines
on the blackboard, her face sometimes involuntarily appears,
the glimpse—more than a glimpse, but brief—not exactly
into her loneliness and exhaustion and despair, but of her
looking into the pool of it, as if she were studying nanocrystals
or polymers. A vision I seemed to want to conjure
not to mock but to qualify, to put in its place—though
the idea is still vivid to me—what I suppose a person should
be able to do. Sheet lightning. A burst of it. A summer field.
And the mirror—the seeing what's there, or some of it,
a light purely reflective, proposing no order in particular.

SMOKING IN HEAVEN

Watching young poets in the early evening
Smoking on the terrace outside the poetry reading,
I wondered if there would be a smoking terrace
In heaven. I have a friend, dead now,
A Catholic who was unimpressed by the prospect of paradise
Until he discovered a group of medieval theologians
Who had proposed that there was a special kind of time
In eternity. They gave it a Latin name.
Like my friend, they couldn't conceive of a God
Who would force them to live forever
Without sunrise and sunset. His wife, a skeptic,
Called it decaffeinated time, at which he shrugged wryly,
This idea of life after death made him very happy,
Which was, as far as he was concerned, the point.
He's been dead now for almost a decade,
So I suppose he knows one way or another
Whether there is nothing after death and no one there
To know it or not. The smoking terrace would, of course, be out of doors,
So it wouldn't be as depressing as those smoking rooms in airports
Where people with grey skin submit to their addiction
With religious humility. You could light up and walk to the edge of the clouds
And watch the fragrant smoke you were expelling
Drift into the decaffeinated sunset. It made me wonder
If there were coffee in heaven. Or sex. I knew a woman
Who said that the main reason for sex,
As far as she was concerned,
Was the cigarette afterward. And if there were sex
In heaven, why would there be anything else? Probably
So that you could also watch Canada geese settle on a lake
Just as the moon was twilighting the surface of the water
In luminous little scallops. The young poets

Should read Allen Ginsberg who said that poets should set an example
By not submitting to what he called "the nicotine haze
Of capitalism." Probably in the heaven without tobacco
The couples are walking by the sea, having already made love,
And the moon, almost unnaturally large, is just coming up,
And the color of the moon on the water is just like what
Their bodies are feeling, contented but still tingling,
And in the moonlight they can see a pack of feral goats
With their beards and inhuman eyes grazing on the hillside, also contentedly,
As if time and eternity were the wrong ideas altogether,
And the women would have come in with their Greek masks on
To walk the shoreline and dance what fate is.

DREAM IN THE SUMMER OF MY SEVENTY-THIRD YEAR

I am behind a funeral cortege on a mountain road
And decide to pass it, but it seems to go on forever
And I'm completely exposed in the oncoming lane
And the only way out is to merge into the caravan
Of mourners. It is getting dark and a thick snow
Begins to fall in a sudden flurry and then stops
Abruptly, which gives the world an expectant air,
Though, really, nothing in particular happens
After a snowfall, except for the intense stillness
In the pine forest the road is winding through.

LOS ANGELES: AN ANALYSIS

"If you think about it, it does seem a special grace.
Of course other animals can do it. Crows, God knows,
find their way to each other every evening.
But here in this city which can seem like nothing
but a maze of freeways. Think of this valley—
it's just the dry riverbed of some ancient river
grown from a little northernmost outpost
of the Spanish empire, the whole thing over time
rationalized with names and streets and freeway loops
and traffic lights and signs—it's just a piece of earth
gathered to this incredibly intricate arrangement
of cross purposes—have you ever wondered why L.A.
produces so many mystery stories? It's because the city
is the mystery—and, anyway, in the midst of it
one man writes a note to another saying
'I'd like to meet you' and the other agrees
and they specify a location—they have these maps
in their heads like crows—and they get into their cars
in quite different parts of the city, and they do,
they arrive at the same place at the same time
and they like each other, oh, immediately.
My friend Sharon asked me recently what love is.
Outrageous, I know. I said, of course, that I didn't know
but that I knew it was a verb. Nouns are another story
entirely. And I suppose that's why 'disappointment'
Is such a useful and delicious word. And like all useful words,
cruel. Still, it doesn't mean the appointment wasn't kept."

OKEFENOKEE: A STORY

"We were in a swamp on the Georgia coast near Folkston,
doing a population survey, which is pretty sketchy work."
A slow drawl: we're lying on a raft in the middle
of a flooded quarry up on the Cumberland Plateau.
Late afternoon in Tennessee, one blue heron in the shallows,
old live oaks festooned with moss. My companions
are telling wildlife ecologists' versions of war stories.
"The only way you can tell a male from a female alligator,"
he was saying, as the water lapped and rocked us,
"is by digital inspection, so my buddy Dwayne—his wife
had just left him and I've seen a soberer man than he was
that day—rammed his hand into the cloacal fold
of the biggest goddam gator you've ever seen.
We had her pinned and tied pretty good, but she's thrashing
seriously, we are all sweating seriously, and the odor
is not inconsiderable, and Dwayne is in up to his forearm
yelling 'Hold 'er! Hold 'er! Just a minute. It's a male!'
And he pulls his hand out and his wedding ring is gone,
and he just stares at his hand a minute and we just sit there
staring at him because we had held that gator
about as long as we were inclined to do, but, of course,
we also knew the decision was up to him."

FOR CECIL, AFTER READING *OHIO RAILROADS*

Thinking about Cecil and trains,
   I thought of the Southern Pacific out of Chicago
      at midnight, winter of 1971,

and the guy in the club car just before it closed
   back from Vietnam and working
      in a slaughterhouse in Kansas City

to which he was returning. He'd had a few, showed me
   his hands, "Fucking cow blood," he said,
      "you can't get it out completely,"

though his open palms looked unsplotched—
   what is the word? "incarnadine"?—
      to me; the little winking lights out the window

in the dark was the headlight of the locomotive
   glowing in the eyes of jackrabbits
      stock still on the winter prairie

as we hurtled south toward Albuquerque.

JERSEY TRAIN

One syllable. When the mind goes groping
for a thing to pray to.
     The refineries
are emitting some gas into the winter dark
and it's flaring in the wind,
as if it were the pilot light of the world,
as if everything were burning at its own rate in the dark
and icy cold.
     The passenger is tired.
She's nodding off, and when she touches her forehead
to the window it's so cold
it hurts and wakes her up.
     And the light
from outside that flickered across her face
made me think of the dark in its orderly fashion
falling across the continent hour by hour and this is
where you need to help me with the bodies,
the curl of young bodies and the sweet breath,
the bedrooms above the garages where the children
lie sleeping, the ones who are safe,
who in the morning have the sliding glass doors that open to the back yards
and the woods beyond.
     Some of them will wake
to totter on two legs, learning the astonishing feat
of walking. Some are sleeping with stuffed animals,
a baseball glove. None of them may become one of the men
who, in their great-grandparents' generation,
sold frozen fruit-ice at the public lynchings.
Or the terrified one summoning resignation,
letting the tension in his body give up
or a frantic rage explode in him
as the crowd gathers.

                    Secret, my country
Is ill. Thinking of the children, who,
whatever else they are, are the future, I thought
of light on water. Flakes of it
flickering and gleaming on the surface of dark water,
or streams of it rilling and braiding over rock
in early light. Light in light, because burning
comes from the sun, but seeing
comes from a spring in us somewhere
near the beginning, somewhere west
of where the dark falls.
                    Shallow light
was the phrase the syllable started
at the cold of the window. Scalloped or flaked,
touching everything, touching it lightly.

SUNGLASSES BILLBOARD IN TERMINI STATION

It covers an entire wall in the cave of the entry hall.
I don't know what the term of art is for each polarized lens
in a pair of glasses, but each glass in the pair of glasses
on the six-foot-high faces on the wall is gleaming.
The head of the young man with the sun-bleached hair
the color of river gold is tilted down and sideways.
The tawny blond woman and the raven-haired man,
raven in breeding season, his sweptback hair glowing
like the lights in the lenses of the glasses
they are wearing, are looking upward and away, not
too far away. They are meant to be wondered at,
rather than arrested in an attitude of wonder. And
isn't that the point? Watching the hooded crows,
in the garden of the Villa Aurelia, with their physical shape
of pure attention, I wondered what they did with themselves
when they didn't need to be attentive, since in the luxury
of that garden and its golden fruits they didn't need to forage.
And thought: they preen. Of course, they preen! They peck
the oily glands at the root of their feathers and spread oil
on the feathers with their beaks. It made me understand
what I was seeing in the vast, dark Plato's cave of the station.
If you knew what creatures chose to do with their leisure hours,
you'd know, beyond necessity, the meaning of the world.
The crows were shopping for sunglasses. Life didn't begin
when the first cell divided, it began when the first two-celled
creature spruced up. It explained Rome to me—people
have been shopping for sunglasses for two thousand years—
though not the mendicant old and infirm slumped against the wall
below the sign on whom had devolved another set of thoughts—
because the point is to look cool, and also to allow the eyes

to withstand the sudden brilliance of the light when you emerge
and stare up at the great stony hive of the Colosseum
above which, over the sounds of a thousand motorbikes,
you can still almost hear the astonished gasps of the crowd.

THREE DREAMS ABOUT BUILDINGS

In the second dream I had taken asylum
In Ely Cathedral to avoid being prosecuted
For a crime I had not committed. In the dream
I had a poignant sense of my innocence—
I was a young father, I had responsibilities,
And I could visualize how appealingly
I could have, given the chance, pled my case
But I was alone in the vast, cold, echoing church
With its smell of candlewax and the police
Were closing in, to arrest me, but also to save me,
Because they were sure I would kill myself
Rather than be taken. It was raining hard
And the fens around the cathedral had flooded
And the cathedral grounds become an island
That could only be reached by digging a ditch
And draining the swirling fen waters. A crew
Had been set to work under massive arc lights
And I could see the harried, middle-aged policeman
Who was supervising, his hair slick with the rain,
And there was one strong man, bald, powerfully
Muscular, shoveling mud calmly, methodically,
With what seemed absolute patience and in the dream
I knew I was him. There was a woman in the third dream,
A beautiful woman, dressed in linens, my wife,
A house full of French doors, many windows
And plants, everything painted white. Across the room—
We were giving a party—I saw her glance my way
And give me a conspiratorial smile. She knew
I wanted to be writing, was composing a pleasant

And attentive face to listen to the group
Of friends I was in. She set down her wine glass
And walked across the room and gave me a kiss
On the cheek, slightly maternal, just below the ear.

PERTINENT DIVAGATIONS TOWARD AN ODE
TO INUIT CARVERS

Because it resembles a sphere, meaning a figure on which every point of its surface is equally distant from its center,

But is a physical object, not a sphere, because as a practical matter an actual physical object cannot be constructed which has a surface every point of which is equidistant from its center,

Pablo Neruda may have missed an opportunity in failing to address an ode to the softball,

Asexual moon of summer nights, the something-to-hit that initiates an intricate ballet of chance- and rule-governed behavior on summer afternoons,

(And for that matter he missed the soccer ball, known in the civilized world as the football, which may have been, as a thought, more culturally available)

(And, Octavio Paz, why did you keep your silence on the almost perfectly round stones that are still to be found lying around the ball courts in Aztec ruins?)

(Hot day, the tar-and-vanilla scent of dry summer grasses, the blue-bellied lizards so still on the stone walls they seemed to be listening to the roar of crowds from Montezuma's last weeks diminishing in the distance like a train whistle)

(And, Pura López, you were wrong to propose in the journalists' bar in Mexico City, after everyone had had lunch and a couple of caballitos, meaning little horses, meaning shots of tequila served in tiny ceramic cups the blue color of melancholy when it's just beginning to turn the corner and get a hold on itself,

That women only liked to watch baseball, on television and in ball parks, because the uniforms made men's butts pleasant objects of contemplation;

Even the women at our table were outraged by this suggestion, and it's no wonder writers don't get much work done after three o'clock in Mexico City)

(And that night when the weather had cooled, Pura, her crinkly black hair cut boyishly, the shiny and almost perfectly round brown irises of her eyes lifted to heaven, singing the soprano part in a Palestrina motet in an almost intimate baroque church in Cuernavaca, not a trace of irony in her gamin's or angel-gamin's face.)

This could be the preface to an ode circumambulating the softball. Or the polyphonies of Palestrina. Almost perfect is the theme. If Plato could have had his way, if the earth were a sphere, instead of almost a sphere, there would probably not be a wobble in its rotation, and hence no ice ages,

And how would you have gotten through interminable afternoons in the fourth grade if there were no pictures of wooly mammoths and saber-toothed tigers as objects of pleasant contemplation in geography books?

(And while we are on the subject, have you noticed that there are never any pictures of ice-age dinosaurs, that there is a profoundly tropical-normative representation of their earthly domain in all the textbooks?)

Ice-age reptiles! We have wandered far from our subject, have we not? Or not? Think of the whiteness of the softball. Imagine a world in which dental and medical care for children were so completely available that all adults, in both hemispheres, had, at least in their twenties and thirties, almost perfectly white teeth.

It implies, doesn't it, a completely different distribution of wealth. That's my point. We are governed by ice-age reptiles.

What if the cycle of oil wars were over, and the undistribution of automatic weapons had commenced, and the wars of distributive vengeance withered away, and the insurrections against grasping dictatorial power rendered irrelevant?

Everyone could be playing or watching softball.

It's only a pop-up, an almost perfectly white day moon of an almost perfectly spherical softball looping through the blue summer air as if it were some sublimely graceful ice-age sea creature riding the ocean of the air,

And she's underneath it looking up, almost as if she were singing a Palestrina motet, the one in which the angel tells the young woman she is full of grace.

The whole spectatorial world has assembled, leaning forward, sipping beer or not, sipping as yet to be invented ginger- and anise-flavored beverage concoctions that our endlessly inventive kind has not yet devised, but with pleasant and familiar fizziness imparted to the nostrils. No one knows yet whether she'll catch it or not. She doesn't know.

But this is a poem in praise of imperfection. Freedom from fear, freedom from violence, and smiles the almost perfect white of the new tusks of an unmolested walrus pup.

This is a poem to old Inuits and the tools they fashioned to fashion dolphins leaping from the lovely pale umber, formerly white, of old ivory.

THREE PROPOSITIONS ABOUT A SUBJECT
STILL TO BE DETERMINED

1.

Grief lives in the old house. The porch
Has not been painted these sixty years
Though there are still, you notice, drops
Of paint the drying process arrested
On the undersides of the cup hooks
That used to hold planters, red geraniums
Against the grey wood all those years ago.
The deaths are waiting in the living room
And you will need to walk past them, you'll need
To show some resolve and walk past them
Because your task is to empty the room
Where the newspapers had accumulated.
You'll recognize it by the smell
Of old paper and the empty dog dish.
Years and years of old newspaper
Bound by twine into bundles, the sinking
Of the *Lusitania,* men walking on the moon.

2.

You have to get up off your knees.
Your medical records aren't the issue
Here. It's true that you could have been
Treated better by various people
On various occasions and that is,

Needless to say, the two-way street
On which you are going to take the test
On the four freedoms, and you can't
Recall now which is the first, freedom
From want or freedom from fear.
You remember the classroom clock
And the wooden desk with its groove
For holding pencils. You are certain
That the third one is freedom of speech.
It seemed logical to you then. First,
Something to eat, and then no power
Out there to terrorize you. Or maybe
You should be safe first, and then fed.
And there's a fourth, but you don't
Remember it at all. Medicine maybe.

3.

Some of them are out watching birds
In the summer morning, or sleeping.
There's a sewing machine store
In the ruined town and it contains
Rows on rows of broken machines
Some of them made dresses on. You
Just stand there and I'll measure. And
In the sporting goods store the smell
Of old leather and neat's foot oil
Is so strong some of them have gathered
To weep. Toss it here. Atta baby.
This was the restaurant. You ate
In booths or at the counter in a chair
That swiveled. There was a picture

On the menu of a large jolly man
With a moustache like bird's wings.
Your father had Yankee pot roast
And your mother had filet of sole.
I'll have the usual, your father said.

FEBRUARY NOTEBOOK: THE RAINS

In the days when I used to hunt ducks the season always ended on the last day of January and on that day we usually hunted until it was too dark to see, so there was something poignant about the moment when the sun sank below the horizon and the sky turned rose and the last ducks— mostly mallards and canvasbacks and widgeon and cinnamon teal at that time of year—headed south, it seemed reluctantly, for their winter feeding grounds in Mexico, wavering skeins of them disappearing from sight as the dark took them. Some genius at the beginning of the last century had planted Japanese plum trees all over the Berkeley hills, the plums whose blossoming in Japanese poetry is always a symbol for the earliest, icy coming of spring. And the Berkeley weather suited them because every year by the middle of February the streets floated in pink and white, mostly pink, blossoms that seem to hang in the air in a gelid and delicate balance until one of the hard rains of that season came straight off the Pacific and took them down. If it happened early the trees were briefly bare again. If it happened late, the new leaves had already begun to make a coppery sheen just as the air was getting milder and the bright red flowering quinces had also begun to blossom. One year, after I'd watched the ducks disappear, and was driving home and came to my street which involved cresting a small hill, my headlights caught in a flash a glimpse of the first plum blossom on a bare tree. Last duck, first blossom. And the days were getting longer.

——

At the Gym

Each body
odd or beautiful, odd
and beautiful, in its own way.

—

Hard rain slapping the window,
lashing the window,
waves of it, coming off San Francisco Bay
and the Pacific beyond, as if to say
I'm energy, I'm here.
and when the sky clears,
rainwater runneling down the leaves of the oaks,
dripping from the leafing-out hydrangea.

—

February: Question

What is older than desire?
the bare tree asked.
Sorrow, said the sky.
Sorrow is a river
older than desire.

—

February is the month of purification.
We don't have that festival.

—

A Memory

The large, cheerful eyes of the yellow duck
on your daughter's rainboots
staring up at you
from the floor of the entryway
near the kitchen.

—

Purification: the desire
for the cessation of desire
is a desire.

—

An Observation

The old art historian—
I don't see him at the gym
    anymore

Or maybe—

The old art historian—
I don't see him at the gym
    these mornings

—

Song

I used to see her at the track,
Her streaming hair, her straight, straight back,
And she became a thought of mine.
St. Valentine, St. Valentine.

Soft her lips and drink the wine.
Her soft, soft lips and sip the wine.
St. Valentine, St. Valentine.

—

Aiglets

They wear out.
You use spit for a while
and then buy new ones.

—

Fog Burning Off

On this grey day what does the morning
say to the afternoon? "Here," it says.
"Here" is what the morning says to the afternoon.

—

Morning: Mid-month

Pink sky at dawn,
and a moth-white moon
just past full.

—

The Usefulness of Sitting Still

The old maple chair by the window
(even in the Trump administration)
gleams a little in the winter sun.

—

Note

Lagunitas Creek, after the long rains,
is the color of café au lait:

one redheaded, orange-beaked merganser's
wake rippling in the milky water.

—

February Question

What is the great good? asked the rain.
Children. Children are a great good,
said the foaming gutters.
                        And the seasons?
asked the puddles in the street mirroring
the passage of the clouds.
                        No,
said the rain. The present, said the rain
and bore down, raindrops
leaping from raindrops on the street.

—

Grand Canyon in February

Rust and rose and salmon pink, pale gold,
tobacco brown,
                    and from deep in the canyon
gusts of icy air, and a silence
unimaginably old.
                    And then the sharp calls
Of a pair of crows riding the updraft
       In the winter sun.

SUMMER STORM IN THE SIERRA

The world goes silver when a storm comes up—
a sudden silvery green.

Not sure what the verb is for cottonwoods
in a princeling wind.

Their trunks never seem to stand so still as when the leaves
leap and shudder on their stems.
Shiver on their stems.

The pines, a darker, inkier green than an hour ago
when their shiny needles were consorting with first light,
driven rain not yet leaping off the pond,
the wind not yet amusing itself
by juddering the aspens,
know what they know and hardly move at all,

the trunks rock faintly, the branches
wave very slightly, as if to acknowledge an embassy
from some inconsequential vassal state. It's late—
or the early part of late—in the ancient world
to which they belong and in which they seem invulnerable,
which, of course, they aren't, being absolute masters
of their weather, but not the climate.

HOTEL ROOM

White walls, clean angles
   got from modernism—
      —form is function! Walter Gropius,
   Weimar 1922.

The craftsmen who apply the thin layer
   of mottled plaster to the sheetrock
      to give the bare walls texture
    are called "mudders."

Clean angles, white walls—
   the effect (imagined almost
     a hundred years ago)
    is orderly and calm.

And in a plain white frame
   on one wall a monotype print
      of three fossil ferns
    "the oldest fossils of land plants

Visible to the naked eye
   were found in Ireland
      and date from the middle Silurian"
    —ferns came later, carboniferous

And bilaterally symmetrical
   as if to invent the possibility
      of being orderly and lyrical at once,
    as if, before mammals, to have

Invented wings. On another wall
    Picasso's *Don Quixote*. Really,
        It's just a few squiggles
        of black paint on paper.

One circular movement of the hand
    for a sun, a quick dash for the horizon
        —the great Don is three strokes
        he's on a horse, a couple of strokes more,

And Sancho, the body
    as credulous servant
        to the soul, is an amiable blob
        the same shape as the sun.

The windmill in the distance
    is desire, I suppose,
        but it's a long way off
        and the riders are in no hurry.

LARGE BOUQUET OF SUMMER FLOWERS,
OR ALLEGORY OF THE IMAGINATION

For Chen Li

You can walk only a finite number of dogs
On a given morning. Say, twelve. Six leashes
In each hand. Or six in one hand, five in the other,
If one of the leashes is that bifurcated kind
For the twin bulldogs. I don't know if it's odd
In Mandarin or Slovakian to call dogs twins.
It's because humans usually give birth
To one of their kind at a time that a pair
Is slightly unusual and the word "twin" in English
Has an odd radiance and, though it can be subtle,
These human pairs walk through the world
As if they are the beneficiaries and victims
Of a luminous mirroring. And since dogs
Can have numerous offspring—we say "litter"
In English, there must be a Russian word
And it must also extend across the mammal species—
A litter of pigs, of cats—applying the faintly spooky
Aura of twinning to dogs doesn't seem quite right
(Though a French psychiatrist has applied it
To consciousness, arguing that we are haunted
Or even constituted by the teasing awareness
Of the presence in ourselves of an unreachable
And twinned other which creates the small shock
We feel when we sense the dissimilarity in metaphors
And in the way that a translation doesn't feel like a twin.)
Imagine you were walking down a lane

In an English village full of half timber houses
With thatch roofs and a rectory by the churchyard
With dormer windows and a melancholy yew.
Just beyond it, in the most nondescript part
Of the walk is an old wooden door, much worn
But newly painted, that leads to a secret garden.
If you imagined the door is blue, you will marry twice.
I'm so sorry for the way your first marriage went.
If you'd had some idea of who you were,
You might at least have made a better job of it.
But remember also the waking early with him or her
Beside you in those first mornings in summer?
If you imagined the door was orange, your daughter
Will marry a fishmonger. Hard, I know, to imagine
That those small deft hands that you loved so much
As they busied themselves with paper snowflakes
Are red and raw from years of being plunged in ice,
But she has grown used to the startled eyes
Of dead sturgeon. Her husband is Italian, something
Of a hothead, but basically a good guy, and
They make a nice living, can afford lessons
For the kids, travel. In fact, at this moment they are sitting
At a white table in a café on a hilltop in Umbria,
Drinking a small cup of strong coffee, looking
Out over olive groves, and feeling, each of them,
Though they may not say it in so many words,
That they are having their lives. It might be
A little hard to explain the expression "in so many words"
In any number of languages, so it may be best
To skip over it, though I am sure there is an equivalent.
If you imagine the door is red, your oldest son's daughter
Will become the mayor of a quaint fishing village
On Puget Sound. She got the likeability gene
That eluded your son. She has three children,

Has mastered the vocabularies of field hockey
And soccer, is widely respected in town and great at budgets.
That's her in the raincoat walking on the old fishdocks
By the harbor mouth. She's too busy and, in truth,
Too unreflective for psychotherapy, but it's where she goes
Sometimes to think about her father whom she loved very much
Despite whatever you may have heard on that score.
There's a watercolor gold on the river's face. Can you say
In Spanish that a river has a face? Hers is a piercing sorrow
She shakes off with a little half-conscious shudder
And a shrug of her shoulders. Walking back to the office,
She passes that woman who walks dogs. Faintly ludicrous.
She's got two black Labs on one fist, a golden retriever,
A wiry little terrier that seems to think it's immense,
And on the other a Dalmatian, a pug-faced Pomeranian,
And a pair of milk-white bulldogs. Many wagging tails,
Much excitement, much voluptuous sniffing of assholes.
Your granddaughter is smiling to herself at how much
This other woman looks like her, is almost identical to her.
It's begun to drizzle so she turns her collar up. She's noticed
That the dog walker is pregnant and smiles thinking
Everyone has to find a way to a living. She isn't thinking,
Of course, that the dog walker is an egregious liar.
She wouldn't. She tends not to see the world that way.

NATURE NOTES 2

> *Two seedling fir,*
> *One died. Io! Io!*
> —GARY SNYDER

One brown-headed cowbird amid the blackbirds
In their iridescent breeding plumage.
Can't mate but there's safety in a flock.

The morning air is "all awash with angels,"

I.e., seeds of the cottonwood drifting in the sun.
The bits of cottony fluff floating on the mild morning breeze
And tumbling a little in the currents of it,
Hundreds of them, thousands, that the sun ignites,
Brightening the air above a drab blackbird juvenile,
Its mouth open so wide you can see
The sunset orange of its throat.
And an adult bird ambulates over
In that blackbird-Egyptian-frieze strut
And pops something in its mouth.
A bit of a worm, I assume,
Or a shiny little beetle going about its shiny beetle business
Until a moment ago.

People study everything. The excrement
Of beetles. The sonic niches of the blackbird's song.
And the sexual excesses of the cottonwood
Which pours thousands of seeds into the air.
So I know that for one to germinate, it has to alight

In moist, sandy soil. A sandbar in the curve
Of a little alpine creek would be just right.
It's a very slim chance, so the tree only exists,
Persists, because it is extravagant. The liver-covered mushrooms
Under the pines are the fruiting bodies of fungi
That send their roots fairly deep into the earth
Where they devour nematodes (microscopic
Animals like worms: humans study everything)
To feed themselves. Don't know
What the nematodes eat, but it must be eating
All the way down until it becomes electricity
And tingles to be tingling.

The morning air is all awash with angels.

Information from a morning lecture: we have gotten so good
At getting soldiers' bodies from the battlefield
To the hospital that a soldier can lose both legs and an arm
And survive, writing notes to the nurses
Because his throat is also ripped out.

Last night's reading: a poet describing her alcoholic uncle
Who didn't take care of himself and died too young.
He was the one, she said, who saw her and knew her.
She wrote some lines about this first adult sadness.
He liked reading about the stars, teaching her the constellations,
This kind man who wrecked himself, who seemed not
To be able to do anything about it. She watched him die,
Loved him helplessly. A poet's task to find the words,
Though perhaps, she said, by writing about something else,
Maybe the night sky, maybe Lyra or the Bear.

This morning the pond is reflecting bankside willows.
The breeze rustles the willow branches,
Ruffles the surface of the water
And produces a dark green, light green, willowy wash
Of a yellow-green watercolor color
Across the pond underneath the dazzled air.

ANOTHER BOUQUET OF SUMMER FLOWERS,
OR ALLEGORY OF MORTALITY

One iris upright in a clear glass vase
And tulips, seven of them,
Peach-colored petals, and the green cascade
Their overheavy heads make
As they droop. Which doesn't seem the right word
For the way those flowers in that vase
Lean there in a tangle of green stems and green sheath-like leaves
That resembles a fall of hair. A luxury of hair. This is a drought year,
So what you notice is the water,
The clear water in the clear vase
Which is on a windowsill. There's a green pond beyond it,
Low this year, the creekside willows
Doubled in the water and the surface of the water very still.
It's a windless morning. Almost July.
Behind the pond grasses climbing toward the bare grey rock
Escarpment of the mountain. The water so precious now
I thought of those Dutch painters of still lifes who excelled
At painting beads of water on the plants.
I imagined one in his somewhat cramped studio in the morning.
He's got a commission to finish. He loves exhibitions
When the crowds lean in to his paintings, exclaiming
At how life-like the small, round, almost shimmering prisms
Of the water drops appear. He's been working for hours now.
He can smell the spicy odor of sausages grilling in the kitchen
As he daubs a water bead onto the petal of a blue hydrangea.
We need water and won't be getting it till winter
When snow begins falling in a fast flutter
Onto the pond and the mountainside,
Falling fast and then faster, thickly,
In a white blur that seems to erase the pond, the mountain.

JOHN MUIR, A DREAM, A WATERFALL, A MOUNTAIN ASH

I had been given two pieces of writing to read.
One was a description of my childhood kitchen
in which, beneath the calm and orderly prose,
something was beating frantically against the walls
like a trapped bat. The other piece contained a small door
you could actually crawl through. It led to the ridge
of a canyon from which you could look down
into an orchard. I knew it was Canyon de Chelly,
knew Kit Carson and his scouts would be coming
to destroy the fruit trees which were neatly aligned
along irrigation ditches that the Spanish called *aquecia*.
Woke feeling nauseous—my wife's soft breathing
beside me. Outside the immense Sierra dark and silence,
a sky still glittering with a strew of stars, a faint brightening
to the east. You'd think, past sixty or so, the unconscious
would give you some respite. But here, it says,
is the little engine of dread and sorrow that runs your story.
And here, almost symmetrically, is the unspeakable cruelty
of the world. In an hour the market in Tahoma will open.
I can drive through the sugar pines. Get coffee,
get a paper. The plan today is to climb Ellis Peak
to see if we can't find the clusters of golden berries
on the mountain ash that we saw last year where the slope
of the trail flattens and the creek runs in a silver sheet
across slabs of granite and then flares into spumes
of white water that leap down the canyon
in what John Muir thought was joy or its earthly simulation.
A good walk, mostly uphill. We can wear ourselves out with it.

AFTER XUE DI

A car bombing in a village in Syria, thirty-seven people, all civilians, dead, fifty or so injured.

The attack "caused the destruction of a large number of houses and buildings in the village," the report said. It was "a government-held village" and something called the Islamic Front, described as "an umbrella for several radical Sunni groups," was said to "claim responsibility" for the bombing. They posted a video of the explosion. It's the rush to own the killings that made something in me just want to quit morally.

I say car bomb, but apparently it was a truck, filled with three tons of explosives which they had to get hold of, pack in the truck—somebody had to know how to do it—instructions available on the internet, also instructions for how to detonate the explosives by calling a timer with a cell phone—somebody had to do that—in what state of mind? 160,000 people have been killed by car bombs in Syria since the insurrection began, so there must be experts with a certain pride in their expertise, the others standing around watching admiringly; or it may have been a young man new to the task, others kibbitzing nervously in the early morning heat, his mind wholly absorbed—"measure twice, cut once," the carpenter's rule applies to the kind of methodical care required of any dangerous physical task. And somebody had to drive the truck, maybe a group, probably whatever looked most ordinary, a couple of guys in a truck, and plant it where the people—it was night when the blast went off, that was why the Islamic Front could post the video of the distant explosion igniting the night sky. The village must have been Shia or Alawite. I imagine that in Syria, as in Iraq and Afghanistan, they have had to develop a sanitary regimen for gathering the body parts after, squads appropriately dressed and wearing those white face masks that are used in hospitals. I think they are called surgical masks.

I thought of Humpty Dumpty—"All the king's horses and all the king's men"—and that sanitary crews, picking hands, feet, less identifiable gobbets of muscle and skin, with special gloves, lifting maimed torsos into body bags and shoveling the intestines in after, are the king's horses and the king's men, the ones who can't sew it together again.

One of Xue Di's prose poems begins, "Mama, let's go float paper boats on the water. When you were small did you also fold paper to make boats?" I would like to introduce, without sentimentality, if that's possible, one of my children, at say age four or five, still sucking on a thumb, but only just at bedtime, and looking at the large book of Mother Goose with peaceful attention and what seems a kind of rapt neutrality, though it may just be that he is about to go to sleep. Staring at the alarmed face of the large egg in a waistcoat which has just lost its balance and listening—not to the moral, exactly, but to the observation. Something the child already must have known, but it is good to have these things said: couldn't put Humpty together again.

Children a little younger than that, still in high chairs, like to drop plates and glasses on the floor experimentally. My children, after the plate or glass had shattered, as it sometimes did, would say "Uh-oh." Not as an expression of concern but as a statement of fact.

You would think people would rush to claim not having murdered large numbers of people living "in the reality of ordinary everyday life." What I think, of course, is that they are sick fanatics, not warriors. Easy for me to say from the comforts of the imperium on a summer night. On the evening in fact of the summer solstice. Can't have been far from the village where the astronomers of Nebuchadnezzar worked out the grand movement of the heavens and invented the 360-day year.

Insert here a long argument about asymmetrical warfare. It's quite possible that the contrivers of that slaughter were not amateurs. The designer of it may have been some Sunni Iraqi officer from the army the United States disbanded, somebody with a Ph.D. in engineering who reads books of guerilla warfare.

"My holy of holies," Chekhov wrote, a doctor, when he was asked about his religious and political convictions, "is the human body."

In 1982 in Hama the Syrian army—the army of the father of the current Syrian dictator Assad—massacred a thousand Sunnis who had risen against his government.

The village of Hora is near the city of Hama, once famous for its water wheels, seventeen of them, the earliest dating back to Byzantium.

Water wheels seem to have been invented in Egypt: "A papyrus dating from the 2nd century B.C. found at Faiyum mentions a water wheel used for irrigation." They must have been constructed from wood. The people in the village must have loved watching the woodworkers, and the wheels would have been constructed with mortise and tenon joinery. I don't know whether they would have used conifer for lightness or oak for strength. The options—there are not many forests in Syria—might have been *Cedrus libani,* cedar of Lebanon, or *Quercus calliprinos,* the Palestine oak.

There is a British human rights organization in Syria documenting or attempting to document the violence. At some considerable risk. And the dead need to be buried, and remembered. It's not as if nothing can be done. The imagination doesn't have to give up.

There are those thirty-seven people, shopping, I suppose, drinking tea in a café. The agendas of their particular lives making electrical signals inside the fleshy brains that were about to be reduced to pulp.

The oldest archaeological evidence of the appearance on earth of our species is ritual behavior at grave sites. There are ways of not quitting morally. From the beginning we knew to tend the dead.

A child's skeleton preserved in the peats of the Ukrainian prairie. The curved horns of sheep arranged around the small body.

DANCING

The radio clicks on—it's poor swollen America,
Up already and busy selling the exhausting obligation
Of happiness while intermittently debating whether or not
A man who kills fifty people in five minutes
With an automatic weapon he has bought for the purpose
Is mentally ill. Or a terrorist. Or if terrorists
Are mentally ill. Because if killing large numbers of people
With sophisticated weapons is a sign of sickness—
You might want to begin with fire, our early ancestors
Drawn to the warmth of it—from lightning,
Must have been, the great booming flashes of it
From the sky, the tree shriveled and sizzling,
Must have been, an awful power, the odor
Of ozone a god's breath; or grass fires,
The wind whipping them, the animals stampeding,
Furious, driving hard on their haunches from the terror
Of it, so that to fashion some campfire of burning wood,
Old logs, must have felt like feeding on the crumbs
Of the god's power and they would tell the story
Of Prometheus the thief, and the eagle that feasted
On his liver, told it around a campfire, must have been,
And then—centuries, millennia—some tribe
Of meticulous gatherers, some medicine woman,
Or craftsman of metal discovered some sands that,
Tossed into the fire, burned blue or flared green,
So simple the children could do it, must have been,
Or some soft stone rubbed to a powder that tossed
Into the fire gave off a white phosphorescent glow.
The word for *chemistry* from a Greek—some say Arabic—
Stem associated with metal work. But it was in China
Two thousand years ago that fireworks were invented—

Fire and mineral in a confined space to produce power—
They knew already about the power of fire and water
And the power of steam: 100 B.C., Julius Caesar's day.
In Alexandria, a Greek mathematician produced
A steam-powered turbine engine. Contain, explode.
"The earliest depiction of a gunpowder weapon
Is the illustration of a fire-lance on a mid-twelfth-century
Silk banner from Dunhuang." Silk and the silk road.
First Arab guns in the early fourteenth century. The English
Used cannons and a siege gun at Calais in 1346.
Cerignola, 1503: the first battle won by the power of rifles
When Spanish "arquebusiers" cut down Swiss pikemen
And French cavalry in a battle in southern Italy.
(Explosions of blood and smoke, lead balls tearing open
The flesh of horses and young men, peasants mostly,
Farm boys recruited to the armies of their feudal overlords.)
How did guns come to North America? 2014,
A headline: DIVERS DISCOVER THE *SANTA MARIA*
One of the ship's Lombard cannons may have been stolen
By salvage pirates off the Haitian reef where it had sunk.
And Cortés took Mexico with 600 men, 17 horses, 12 cannons.
And La Salle, 1679, constructed a 7-cannon barque,
Le Griffon, and fired his cannons upon first entering the continent's
Interior. The sky darkened by the terror of the birds.
In the dream time, they are still rising, swarming,
Darkening the sky, the chorus of their cries sharpening
As the echo of that first astounding explosion shimmers
On the waters, the crew blinking at the wind of their wings.
Springfield Arsenal, 1777. Rock Island Arsenal, 1862.
The original Henry rifle: a sixteen-shot .44 caliber rimfire
Lever-action, breech-loading rifle patented—it was an age
Of tinkerers—by one Benjamin Tyler Henry in 1860,
Just in time for the Civil War. Confederate casualties
In battle: about 95,000. Union casualties in battle:

About 110,000. Contain, explode. They were throwing
Sand into the fire, a blue flare, an incandescent green.
The Maxim machine gun, 1914, 400–600 small caliber rounds
Per minute. The deaths in combat, all sides, 1914–1918
Were 8,042,189. Someone was counting. Must have been.
They could send things whistling into the air by boiling water.
The children around the fire must have shrieked with delight.
1920: Iraq, the peoples of that place were "restive,"
Under British rule and the young Winston Churchill
Invented the new policy of "aerial policing" which amounted,
Sources say, to bombing civilians and then pacifying them
With ground troops. Which led to the tactic of terrorizing civilian
Populations in World War II. Total casualties in that war,
World wide: soldiers, 21 million; civilians, 27 million.
They were throwing sand into the fire. The ancestor who stole
Lightning from the sky had his guts eaten by an eagle.
Spreadeagled on a rock, the great bird feasting.
They are wondering if he is a terrorist or mentally ill.
London, Dresden. Berlin. Hiroshima, Nagasaki.
The casualties difficult to estimate. Hiroshima:
66,000 dead, 70,000 injured. In a minute. Nagasaki:
39,000 dead; 25,000 injured. There were more people killed,
100,000, in more terrifying fashion in the firebombing
Of Tokyo. Two arms races after the ashes settled.
The other industrial countries couldn't get there
Fast enough. Contain, burn. One scramble was
For the rocket that delivers the explosion that burns humans
By the tens of thousands and poisons the earth in the process.
They were wondering if the terrorist was crazy. If he was
A terrorist, maybe he was just unhappy. The other
Challenge afterwards was how to construct machine guns
A man or a boy could carry: lightweight, compact, easy to assemble.
First a Russian sergeant, a Kalashnikov, clever with guns
Built one on a German model. Now the heavy machine gun,

The weapon of European imperialism through which
A few men trained in gunnery could slaughter native armies
In Africa and India and the mountains of Afghanistan,
Became "a portable weapon a child can operate."
The equalizer. So the undergunned Vietnamese insurgents
Fought off the greatest army in the world. So the Afghans
Fought off the Soviet army using Kalashnikovs the CIA
Provided to them. They were throwing powders in the fire
And dancing. Children's armies in Africa toting AK-47s
That fire 30 rounds a minute. A round is a bullet.
An estimated 500 million firearms on the earth.
100 million of them are Kalashnikov-style semi-automatics.
They were dancing in Orlando, in a club. Spring night.
Gay Pride. The relation of the total casualties to the history
Of the weapon that sent exploded metal into their bodies—
30 rounds a minute, or 40, is a beautifully made instrument,
And in America you can buy it anywhere—and into the history
Of the shaming culture that produced the idea of Gay Pride—
They were mostly young men, they were dancing in a club,
A spring night. The radio clicks on. Green fire. Blue fire.
The immense flocks of terrified birds still rising
In wave after wave above the waters in the dream time.
Crying out sharply, as the French ship breasted the vast interior
Of the new land. America. A radio clicks on. The Arabs,
A commentator is saying, require a heavy hand. Dancing.

1. A Basque Restaurant in Bakersfield

Monday, January 25, 2010

Left Berkeley about one o'clock and drove south,
Then east in a light rain, the hills green,
Mustard flowers—the first sign of spring—an acid yellow
Stain on the hillsides at Altamont Pass.
                        Super Bowl Sunday in America—
There are almost no cars on the road,
We alternately listened to the game and read each other
The *Aeneid* which Brenda is teaching. *Arma*
Virumque cano down Highway 5's agro-desert
Of alternating monocrops, which is in its way
Quite beautiful, acres of grape vines
Pruned so that the plants lie flat on crucifix-shaped racks
To carry, I guess, the weight of the heavy Barbera grapes of the valley.
The vines are purplish in the wet winter
And create a spectacular effect against the orange
And rose of the sun going down behind the Santa Lucias.
Also rows and rows of bare apricot trees,
Also stretching to the horizon, one snowy peak
In the distance, some sheep grazing on hillsides
As the early dark comes on.
                        Stopped
Just after sundown in Bakersfield
At the junction of 58 and 99
And checked into a motel, then drove out
To look for a place for dinner, avoiding the chains,
And came upon a sign for Benji's French-Basque Restaurant
In an old shopping mall. Thought of Frank Bidart's

Golden State. Of course, Bakersfield
Was Basque & thought also of the North Beach restaurants
In my college years—Hotel Du Midi and Des Alpes,
Places where Basque sheepherders from the Eastern Sierra
Were said to crash when they visited the city
And where you could get boardinghouse-style dinners
For $2, $3 if you wanted wine, strong red served in pitchers
That you drank from jelly glasses which you could refill,
As one friend said, as long as you could still stand up.
          Inside a dining room and a bar,
The dining room empty except for one elderly couple
And a few people in the bar watching the last quarter
Of the Saints-Vikings game. Benji, a man about my age
Or older, was behind the bar, grey hair,
A handsome, very Basque face, the flat cheekbones
And the aquiline nose, expressive mouth. He asked
Where we were from, I said the Bay Area,
He said I used to cook in a restaurant on Broadway
In San Francisco in the 1960s. I said, Hotel Du Midi.
He smiled and said, Right! Came down here
Where I had relatives and started this place.
The bartender, a bullet-headed young guy, bald,
With a black goatee had a bet on the Saints
Who appeared to be losing. Benji (and Brenda)
Were rooting for the Vikings because of their badly battered
Veteran quarterback. The two waitresses with not much to do
Kept coming in to check the score and commiserate
With the bartender. Benji was saying the Du Midi was a scene,
Lenny Bruce used to come in and Miles Davis,
Jack Kerouac. I said, You knew Jack Kerouac?
He said, Jack was a good guy, heart a mile wide.
But he had bad trouble with the bottle. The game
Got turned around on a fumble and the Saints won
In overtime. The bartender—Mike—collected his winnings

From two old guys down the bar and bought us
Each a glass of wine, split the rest with the waitresses.
The older waitress, hair dyed punk black,
Said, You guys better eat while the kitchen's open—
The cook had come out to see what all the shouting
Was about—and we went into the dining room,
He to the kitchen.

              We were served the family-style
Basque spread of forty years ago: first a vegetable soup,
Lots of cabbage in it, with dishes of baked beans,
A spicy tomato roux to be stirred into the soup,
Little Basque white loaves, then brochettes of grilled lamb
With plates of corn, French fries, green salad,
Slices of pickled cow's tongue. Too much
And all of it quite good. The kitchen crew
Had joined the festivities at the bar. Our waitress,
Mikele, was back and forth, comparing alchemical tattoos
With Brenda. Did we want coffee, fresh fruit?
We said thanks, no, a little coffee. Drank it
Said goodnight to Benji, Mike, Mikele. On the tv
The postgame interviews were winding down.
Went back to the Hilton Garden Inn, $99
A night and continental breakfast
       This was the first day.

2. A Straight Shot to Vegas

Tuesday, January 26

Drove out of Bakersfield on Highway 58,
Heading east—the flat valley, acres of citrus groves
Either side of the highway (exactly the shot from *Chinatown*),
Leaves glistening from last night's rain—these are the groves

That the stolen Owens River water brought into being,
That idyl of a golden California—and rose up out of them,
Crossed the Tehachapis through a patchwork of snow
And grey rock, bare valley oaks on the hillsides
Going up and coming down, which were either sick
Or deciduous. Scrub pines near the pass
At about 4500 feet, then the precipitous descent
To a stretch of barren high desert (that the map called Devil's Playground),
Barstow, Mojave, always some snow on distant peaks,
Joshua trees here and there, bursts of some tough,
Scrubby desert plants of the kind that learned to survive
By being leathery and parsimonious (and that put me in mind
Of the English Puritans in New England
Calling some low-growing, salt-afflicted coastal scrub plants "wolves' farts").

A couple of casinos at the state line—
An American equivalent of Stalinist architecture,
Tall rectangles thrown up in no relation
To geography, to which a great deal of dispiriting neon
Was attached like a bad idea of a good time
That made each of the buildings seem lonely and singular
Like elders with memory loss stock still in a parking lot.

Then the straight shot to Las Vegas, though we stopped
At pullouts to listen to the silence
Between sixteen-wheel trucks hauling what must be Chinese goods
To all points east, and to smell the desert
And identify a couple of circling hawks,
High, high up. The desert smelled like salt and alkali and sage
And the hawks, probably ferruginous,
Looked like the freest creatures this part of the world
Knows about.

Got lost for forty-five minutes
In a Las Vegas suburb (called Paradise)—
Brick one-story newish suburban homes
With cacti in the yards or winter-dead lawns.
We picked up our friend Janet Weil at the bus station
Near the old "Strip" downtown, when Vegas was still
A 1950s–'60s idea of Coney Island tourism,
Gift shops and penny arcades. And met Kat Factor
Who'd driven down from Idyllwild and had dinner on the new Strip
In a casino brew-pub with fountains outside gushing water
And inside an oyster bar and kickboxing on all the television sets
And humans of many varieties feeding slots
And showing absolutely no interest in how oysters
Got to the desert or where the water in the gushing fountains
Came from (Colorado River which is stilled to a trickle
At its delta) or why people would want to watch other people
Kick each other in the face.

3. Drones in the Desert

Wednesday, January 27

The lobby and breakfast room of the La Quinta
In North Las Vegas. Sitting over a second coffee to make notes.
Early up, I tried to get into the spirit of the thing
And borrowed Janet's magic markers and made a large sign
That reads VIOLENCE IS ALWAYS WRONG EXCEPT OURS.

North out of North Las Vegas,
The working class end of the money machines and gushing fountains,
A new makeshift suburb turns into Great Basin desert very quickly.
A flat tableland, about 2000 feet above sea level,
Of coyote bush and sage, a hard put soil

In which even the yucca and Joshua tree seem merely occasional,
Ringed by mountains, snowy in the west
And bare eroded rock to the east.
A bleak splendor to the look of things.

The Air Force base sits in a shallow basin
Under a huge blue sky. The base is fenced by chainlink
Topped with circular coils of razor wire. In the distance
Two large beige hangars and a scattering
Of pre-fab buildings, one- and two-story,
All the color of the desert.

The adjacent town—Indian Springs—
Consists of a casino, a small adobe building
With one sign that says STEAK AND EGG BREAKFAST $5.99
And another that says WIN A HARLEY, FOOD, BAR, SLOTS.

Next to the casino an abandoned gas station,
Next to the gas station a small motel done up in Victorian Gothic frontier
And painted bright yellow. Beyond it the remains
Of another abandoned bar with a faded sign
That says EL SUEÑO.

East of the highway, up a hillside, the town
Like any small, inland west boom town—
Is dust, cottonwoods, a scattering of trailer homes
And pre-fab housing. And a sign saying
HOME OF THE INDIAN SPRINGS THUNDERBIRDS.

The sign at the entrance to the base itself says,
In Navajo-looking lettering,
CREECH AIR FORCE BASE HOME OF THE HUNTERS.

Approaching in a car at 7:30 in the morning—
We wanted to arrive before the young men and women
Who piloted the drones came down out of the hillside trailer homes,
Having seen their children, if they had them, off to school—
Was a long line of construction trucks
Lined up by the side of the road
At the commercial entrance to the base—cement trucks
And dump trucks and flatbeds carrying pipes
And cement culverts and construction materials.
Pavers and forklifts. Also delivery vans
And food service six wheelers, one driver
Sitting patiently at the wheel of each truck.

Defense money pouring in to expand the landing strips
Must have been doing well for local businesses.
Stimulus money, they call it. Names
On the trucks: Discount Dumpster, Deli Express (#1 Selling Sandwich!),
Southern Nevada Readymix, Lone Star Construction,
South Nevada Paving.

The drones themselves are startling,
And it takes the brain a moment to produce the reason why.
The bodies from the front are shaped like fighter planes
But the cockpits have no windows, just a blister of black
On the fuselage—because there's no one in it,
No one needs to see out, and halfway back they taper to a sort of tail,
Like a dragonfly's, and the electronics that replace the human eye
Hang from the bodies of the planes like a wasp's legs.

Wasp, dragonfly, they came soaring over the desert basin and the intense
    blue
Of the sky like malignant insects, and they were soundless.

Parked in the casino's empty parking lot.

(Inside the bartender was at the bar—
A woman, maybe early thirties, in a red bow tie—
Had to be a military wife—
Listening to the radio, cleaning the bar,
Not another person in the place
And all the slots and poker machines turned on
And flashing in the casino gloom.)

Some emblem of working life in America,
In many parts of the world.

Walked in the early desert chill down the fence line
To the commercial gate we'd driven past
On the weedy roadside—Brenda, Janet
(Here for the third time and knows the drill),
Kat and me. We could see through the chainlink fence
That security at the main gate explained the long lines,
Each truck and trucker being carefully inspected.

A few cars roared past on the freeway.
Weaving through the creosote-scented scrub
A dark blue pickup from inside the fence
With AF SECURITY painted on its side
Pulled up opposite us to get a good look—
All three of the women were wearing pink which told them
Who we were. (Mostly it's either Catholic Worker people
Or Code Pink.) The truck slowed and then sped up
And proceeded to the gate. (Had they wanted
To intimidate us, they would have tracked us at our pace,
I thought.) ALPHA ALERT flashing on the security screen
At the entrance guard post and, close enough now,

We could see a half dozen to a dozen soldiers in desert fatigues
Checking each big truck as it rolled in.
(Old song in my head: *Up in the morning,*
out on the job, work like the devil for my pay.)

Winter sun rising over the mountains to the east
And turning the sky a milky white, then blue,
And the Joshua trees and desert grasses
Golden in the early light. Two things:
The trucks are the military side of the stimulus—
They are building new landing strips
For the new drones that are being rushed
Into production—military drones cost twelve million dollars
To build, $30,000 an hour to fly—and the heightened security
Must have been a result of the recent bombing
Of a CIA base in Afghanistan, where the drones
Used in Pakistan had done their targeting.
The Afghan drones are said to be targeted from Creech.

Reuters, Jan 2010:
51 drone air strikes in Pakistan in 2009
Killing about 460 people (according
To Pakistani officials); 32 strikes in 2008,
Killing 240 people.

The Economist, 1-14-10:
A Pakistani organization "estimates 667 civilians
Killed by drones in 2009."

The soldiers at the gate glance our way
And keep checking the IDs of the drivers.
We are standing on the unpaved verge of the freeway,
Twenty yards or so from the gate, and visible

To both the truckers and the Air Force personnel
Who are pulling up to their gate in late model Chevies and Hondas.
They must be driving their first cars, many of them,
Bought on first loans from first jobs. Could imagine
The ads on local tv. American flags
And LOW RATES AND NO HIDDEN FEES
Flashing on the screen. Going to work on a Tuesday morning.

A Nevada Highway Patrol cruiser pulls up behind us
And a tall, lean, middle-aged man gets out. "Good morning, folks."
We had our signs out and Kat had begun to read Emily Dickinson
And Wordsworth to the morning air. We said good morning.
"Just here to remind you of the rules. I'm here to protect your rights
And you have the right to stand on the dirt ground and exercise freedom
   of speech.
Standing on the tarmac is trespassing on federal property
And I will have to arrest you. That clear?"
Janet says she's been here often and it's very clear.
He says, "You have a good day," starts to get into his cruiser
And then hesitates. "Would you folks mind telling me
If you're planning to get arrested?" I am about to say we aren't
And Janet says, an edge in her voice,
"We haven't decided." He nods and drives off. I say to Janet,
"We're not getting arrested, right? Why not make his day
A little easier?" Janet says, "We're not here to make their days
Easier." This provokes a brief philosophical and strategic discussion
Among us, and we get our water bottles from our back packs,
Put on more sunscreen, and face toward the incoming cars
And hold up our signs. Kat starts to read Wordsworth again:
"A slumber did my spirit seal. I had no human fears."

Predator drones are built by General Atomics
In Poway, California, near San Diego.

New York Times: "Air Force officials acknowledge that
More than a third of unmanned Predator spy planes (n.b.)
Have crashed, mostly in Iraq and Afghanistan."

Col. Eric Mathewson directs the Air Force task force
On "unmanned aircraft systems." At a congressional hearing:
"I'll be really candid . . . We're on the ragged edge."

The CIA is in charge of drone flights in Pakistan.
The Air Force in Iraq and Afghanistan.
A hundred and ninety-five Predators in the Air Force fleet,
January 2010, and twenty-eight Raptors.
The total number of military drones (including
Tiny, hand-launched models) has "soared to 5,500
From 167 in 2001.

"Most of the crews sit in 1990s style computer banks
Filled with screens, inside dimly lit trailers.
Many fly missions in both Iraq and Afghanistan on the same day."

David Kilcullen, testifying to Congress:
"Since 2006 we have killed 14 senior Al Qaeda officials
Using drone strikes; in the same period,
In the same area, we have killed 700 civilians."

11 A.M. Witness can be a little boring.
I have mostly been holding up my sign
For the cacti and the Joshua trees to read.
Kat's sign reads THERE IS ANOTHER WAY.
We've read, to no one in particular, Marianne Moore
And Gertrude Stein and Langston Hughes.
The sun almost noon high. When there is no traffic
You can hear the desert plants ticking in the heat.

4. Jailbird Priests

Thursday, January 28

Did our morning stint at Creech and then drove north
Past Cactus Springs which seemed to consist
Of an abandoned RV camp and then, amazingly, bright
White and domed, in the brown and tan desert scrub
A temple dedicated to the lionheaded Egyptian goddess
Sekhmet—a retreat center devoted to a neo-pagan form
Of women's spirituality with a priestess in residence.
It has not, Janet said, been active in demonstrations,
But activists camp there and meditate and gather their wits.

Just beyond it is one of the remarkable places in North America,
And there is nothing to see but a series of sturdy wire fences,
A gated entry road, acres of rocky ground, cactus, sage,
And just visible in the distance across the wide empty desert
A complex of buildings. The Nevada Proving Grounds
Renamed the National Nuclear Test Site, and more recently,
The Nevada National Security Site. We stopped, got out,
Walked to the gate, stretched—Brenda pointed out
A Gila woodpecker, elegant creature with a zebra-striped back,
Red head, making a yipping cry as it hopped from branch to branch
In a small Joshua tree. There were a hundred atmospheric tests
Of nuclear weapons in this place in the 1950s and 1960s.
That must have wiped out unimaginable numbers of birds,
Mammals, plants, and insect life. And then wiped them out again
And again. Note to myself to see if studies have been published,
Which seems unlikely. The testing stopped altogether in 1992
So this young woodpecker is among the latest recolonizers
Though there are places in the complex that won't
Be habitable for thousands of years. We read the air

A final set of poems and got into the car—
It was time to turn around and start back.
But we stopped again, at Janet's suggestion, in Las Vegas
To visit the office/crashpad of the Nevada Desert Experience,
The organization that acts as a clearing house for demonstrations
At Creech and the Test Site.
                    Getting on to noon. The house
Was white stucco, one story, in a working class suburban cul-de-sac,
Cactus in the front yard, a small statue of Francis of Assisi,
And a pair of white-blossoming oleander, their sickle-shaped leaves
Drooping in the heat—these are the plants I'd seen
On Crete in the White Mountains near the mouth of a cave
That I was told had once been the home of Aphrodite—
Leave Crete, goddess, Sappho wrote (if Sappho could write)
In the Mary Barnard translation, *and come to this temple*
Dappled by the shadows of apple branches. Something
Like that.
                    Janet had called ahead and Jim Haber,
The director, met us in the driveway. Inside,
The house felt like a fraternity or a student coop
Except for the pictures of Gandhi and Martin Luther King,
Thoreau and Rosa Parks pinned to the walls.
A burly, balding man was talking on a cell phone
in the living room. Sweat pants, t-shirt, flip-flops,
A broad, handsome face. He was the legendary Franciscan,
Father Jerry Zawada. What I knew of him—two years
In federal prison for camping out on top of missile silos
In the Midwest, more jail time for disrupting entry
To the School of the Americas in Fort Benning, Georgia,
Where the U.S. Army taught counterinsurgency
And techniques of "enhanced interrogation"
To the military of Central American dictatorships.
Also for protesting torture training at a military base

In Arizona where he also worked with No Más Muertes,
The group that made food and water drops in the desert
For people risking their lives crossing the border.
Also got censured by the Vatican for saying Mass
With women priests. When he was off the phone,
Jim introduced us. We described our uneventful days
At Creech to which Father Zawada listened with interest
And said someone had dropped off a large bowl
Of strawberries and why didn't we all have lunch
And read poems. We accepted gratefully and he said,
I can offer you Rice Krispies or Cheerios. I chose Rice Krispies—
And while they hustled out bowls and a carton of milk,
Wandered through the rooms and looked at the bookcases—
Thomas Merton, Thich Nhat Hanh, a biography of Dorothy Day,
But also a few novels—Mary Gordon, Toni Morrison.
A bulletin board with notices of demonstrations past.
The strawberries were small, intensely red, and luscious.
And the milk was cold. Father Zawada told us the story
Of one of his adventures at the Nuclear Test Site.
He and another priest, a Father Louie, managed to get
Inside the main gate and scrambled into a culvert
Which took them to the second gate where they took out
Their priest kits and began to say Mass. They didn't get very far
Before security arrived and escorted them to the gate.
"They knew us and didn't bother arresting us and we have
The big gathering next week so we decided not to make an issue
Of it. Louie," he said, "was disappointed. He liked the idea
Of getting busted for committing transubstantiation
On government property." We read poems—Janet read the Dylan
    Thomas poem
She'd read in the desert with a title like a newspaper headline:
"Among Those Killed in the Dawn Raid Was a Man Aged
One Hundred" which had Thomas's huge music
And silenced us for a moment.

Brenda and Father Zawada talked a little about Tucson
Where the local bishop had kicked him out. We bussed
Our cereal bowls, after a while, and said goodbye.
Walked out into the heat. We dropped Kat at her car
In the weird daylight nakedness of downtown Las Vegas
And Janet at the Amtrak station and found our way
To the freeway entrance. Brenda fishes the *Aeneid*
From her bag and I begin to read, as she drives.
End of book six. Aeneas has just emerged from the underworld
Through the gate of ivory and sets sail for the Italian coast.
A long drive home to save the cost of another motel.

SEOUL NOTEBOOK

1. First Day of the Conference on Peace

Arrived at the institute late Friday; it's a graduate school, the Institute of
    Korean Studies.

Early Saturday morning—the campus is in a little town just outside Seoul,
on the southeast side, set among hills. Couldn't see much in the dark
so the morning was a shock: sharp clear air, bright blue sky,
brilliant color in all the trees, golds of beech and chestnut, shiny yellow of
    the gingkos,
flame-red, carmine, and scarlet of the maples, and the orange-red
of some others—horse chestnuts? Anyway, a mid-Picasso's palette—
a mix of gold, flame-orange, new copper, old brass, just stunning,
and mixed with them the dark green of conifers.
The college buildings are modernist versions of traditional Korean
    architecture,
the hills around a more subdued orange-brown, green-and-umber,
a little mist still rising from the night damp
in the crowns of the trees at the top of the hill.

So gorgeous I had a slight sensation of dizziness and nausea walking
    around.

Also broad lawns
and the dramatic Korean magpie, the *gaatchie*,
a crow-sized black bird with white sides and a dark lustrous blue streak
the length of its wings. And a loud cry like the turning of a rusty crank.

What else? In a half hour walk, an egret on a pond,
a bird that looked like a European coal tit, a medium-sized bird,
with a scimitar of orange around its eye and a high-pitched song,

a wild pigeon or dove, brown-grey,
with a look of tessellated tile work or scales on its back.

And—besides the yellow gingko leaves on the paths
and the smear of gingko nuts (putrid-smelling, I've read, but I have a bad
    cold
and couldn't smell it) which people were gathering all along the road
(for breakfast at the hotel a rice gruel with gingko nuts)
the most beautiful thing is the bare persimmon trees seen uphill against
    the sky,
a fretwork of bare branches like brushstrokes,
and randomly, among the branches the bright orange globes
of the persimmons and occasionally
(as in some insanely intense T'ang painting)
one of the *gaatchies* in the tree.

Breathed the air. This country entirely destroyed by war
fifty years ago, the cities reduced to rubble, near-starvation in the villages,
women making a broth of wild grasses every morning
to keep the children from rickets.

The struggle for control of the country after the Japanese were expelled
became the star proxy in the Cold War and visited on the country the full
insensate fury of mid-twentieth-century aerial bombardment. Of course
they would be holding international conferences on the idea of peace.

A beginning. Professor Kim: Is "peace" merely the buzzword of a
    coopted liberalism?
The long wish of the Korean people, a yearning
formed by Korea's hard and bitter history in the twentieth century?

After the Cold War the "clash of civilizations" described by Huntington
seems to be carrying the hope and fears expressed by the dream of "peace."

Wordsworth, Valéry, Eliot—the power of art to communicate among
  peoples,
Blah, blah, blah.

Guy Sorman, French columnist, economist:
Conflicts are always driven by the quest for power.
Ideology is the rationale for why the actors deserve power,
a rationale always radiant to the person or group that espouses it.

Dialogue is not an easy way to peace. Dialogue begins not from politeness
but from the possibility that the other may have legitimate claims, an
attitude that is only bred, often, once violence has exhausted itself. The
question of how to get there before the first sweet dream of retribution
initiates a cycle of violence seems to have eluded human beings. (Getting
this from the on-the-spot English translation of the French talk.)

Why he disagrees with Huntington. More conflicts happen within
than between cultures and civilizations,

Why are religious and civil wars more dreadful? Is tribalism—
the human impulse of affiliation—itself a violence?
An othering in the mind that licenses violence?

Civilization is the subjugation of tribal and ethnic identities.
Is civilization the origin of conflict?
When a civilization decides it is a tribe (Nazi Germany), watch out.

Culture is not violence. A politics need not be violent. The state seeks a
monopoly on violence. The quest for power is the source of violence. Cul-
tures evolve. That's where the daily life that constitutes the inner life of a
civilization gets acted out. It is where ordinary people, nurses, professors,
shopkeepers, may be able to make a difference.

Tea break. The audience is mostly formally dressed, suit and tie.
All the Asians are in suit and tie, the Europeans not so much.
Mostly male, mostly middle-aged. The atmosphere not somber but
   engaged.

We need to talk about Thich Nhat Hanh. We need to talk about engaged
   Buddhism,
Says one man—the only Korean in the room not wearing either monk's
   robes or a suit and tie.

The solemnity of ideology.
What Salman Rushdie was guilty of was laughter.

An agitated man says academics who call other academics "liberal"
mean that the ones doing the name-calling are willing to resort to
   violence
while their timid colleagues aren't. Well, he says, time will tell.

Another man says the desperate are not having conferences about peace.

Will global markets create shared values, an older woman asks,
a Chinese scholar in a very severe and elegant business suit.

Isn't radical Islam the elephant in this room? an Italian guy in a tweed
   sport coat
and an open-collared shirt. Peace,
a white-haired Korean man who is treated deferentially by the Koreans,
is a converging target;
it must come from human diversity and nourish it.

Wander back out into the stunning day. We are to meet Brother Anthony
   this afternoon for a traditional Korean tea ceremony in Insadong.

2. Mouths of Babes

Second day. Deep breath.
Professor Hwa: Civilization is a victory of persuasion over force.

Borders: let us imagine the slow overlapping of cultures
that live together and apart, borrowing from each other,
common interests preserving them from war

(Sounds like a description of marriage—the woman next to me
    muttering)

The world is unfinalizable, an English translation
of a Korean translation of a neologism in Russian of Bakhtin's

Culture is not harmony, it is disagreement short of violence.

Professor Cho: A necessary condition for democracy
is the ability to entertain the possibility
that the other person might be right.

This is also, according to Gadamer, the soul of hermeneutics.

Buber, according to Professor Hwa: too many talkers,
not enough listeners. Good reading
is acute listening. It models
the transformation of otherness
that is the mystery at the heart of ordinary kindness
and also the possibility of a moral life.

(Tea break. A flurry of young women in white shirts and black bow ties
scurry in to this almost entirely male gathering
with trays of porcelain teapots and plates of almond cookies)

Chat with the very beautiful American wife
of the Korean professor of the philosophy of science.
She's from Kansas, looks like an aging Catherine Deneuve.
Their daughter, named Holly, introduced to me as a young poet,
looks like any American kid
until she asks me if I thought Rilke's *Sonnets to Orpheus*
should be translated into English with or without rhyme.

I asked her if she were enjoying the day
and she said it may be the most thrilling of her life.

After that I kept seeing and hearing through my imagination of her eyes,
kept imagining the world as a kind of simultaneous narrative
of everything that happens from an infinitely nuanced and
    overlapping set
of points of view. A beautiful, slightly world-weary woman
from the Middle West married to an academic from Korea,
what is that movie? Their daughter's carefully lacquered, vaguely Gothy
    nails.
The various world, unaccountable finally, that the headphones
and the simultaneous translation seemed to mime.

In the afternoon, philosophers on the relevance of Confucianism.
An old professor from Beijing University: Confucian thought
had only a sense of hierarchy, and not a sense of otherness.
Class consciousness could "other" Confucian thought
and give it dynamism. White hair cut short, a baggy suit,
A sense that there was something vastly humorous
about what he was saying. A slick, earnest Japanese professor
from Narita with heavy black frame glasses,
a very expensive suit, an expert on communication
among (and apparently failure of communication among)
national scientific bureaucracies. I looked to see if Holly was listening.
She seemed enchanted. And, finally, the Korean professor,

her father, who had the impassive face of a man
who had sat through many symposia and kept his own counsel,
delivered a very chiseled and acutely written talk
on whether some apparently controversial nineteenth-century Confucian
   philosopher
was pro- or anti-science, the subtext of which seemed to be
that science was always a progressive force until governments
found it useful, which was when they thought it could improve ways
of controlling or killing people. Delivered not with an air of cynicism,
but of a business consultant making a routine report of the facts.

I took a walk in the break. The sun had come out again
and there had been that morning a light, the lightest dust of snow
on the gold and autumn red of the hills. I decided to skip the panel
on the Korean Wave in film and get a cab back to the hotel.
Holly was coming up the path. I said goodbye, she shook my hand
and said, "We've got to think our way to world peace."
She was wearing a pale turquoise quilted down coat
and a sky-blue scarf and we were standing under one of those starry-
   leaved maples
that made a russet stain on the pond. "The Iranian professor,"
she fished out her notebook to get it right,
"said it's God's will that we are different from each other.
Do you believe that?" I asked her what she believed
and she looked savage. "If there is a God and this is his world, then
   everything is God's will. Hiroshima was God's will. The AIDS
   epidemic in Africa
is God's will." I said, "And is that what you believe?" She consulted her
   notebook
and said, "I believe what Professor Wu said." And she read it to me.
"We are no safer than the most vulnerable among us."

Tomorrow a plane back to Iowa City, two days of clearing out,
and we'd be driving to Berkeley. In five days

I'd be on my way there in the breakfast room of a motel in Kearney,
    Nebraska,
drinking the local idea of coffee and peeling the paper lid off
one of those individually packaged plastic bowls of corn flakes.
There will be American news in the newspapers. Life a set of Russian dolls
or Chinese boxes. A sign saying that wind energy advocates
would be meeting in the Willa Cather Room.

TWO TRANSLATIONS FROM ANGLO-SAXON

1. The Battle at Brunanburh

In that year Aethelstan, thane of thanes,
king, ring-giver, won great glory
in a battle at Brunanburh with the blade of his sword.
Also the *aethling*, his younger brother, Edmund.
They broke the shield wall, hewed linden-boards
with sword edge, hacked them with hammered metal.
They were the sons of Eadward, Alfred's grandsons.
It suited their Saxon birth to spill the blood
of a loathed foe, defending their lands,
their homesteads and horde-goods.
                                    And the enemy was stove through,
the Scotsmen and ship-raiders
fell as if fated. The fields soaked up blood
from first light at morning, when the Lord's star,
the Eternal Lord's bright candle, rose
to glide over earth, till it had gone to its rest,
glorious Being, and left behind bodies
that spears had destroyed, bodies of Norsemen
sprawled on their scutcheons, and the Scotsmen as well,
exhausted and war-gorged.
                                    The men of Wessex
harried them hard while the light lasted,
herded in troops the fugitives fleeing before them
and slashed at them sorely with swords ground sharp.
Nor did the Mercians refuse hard hand-play
to any of the foe who turned to face them
from among the warriors who had followed Anlaf
over the sea surge, crouched in the ship's breast,
to seek out the land they were fated to die in.

Five lay dead on the field of battle, young kings
the sword put to sleep, and another seven
of Anlaf's earls, and an untold number
of shipmen and Scots. And they sent fleeing
the Norsemen's chief. Need drove him
to the ship's prow with what remained of his people.
They pushed out on the tide, took the king out
on the fallow flood-tide, and that saved his life.
Constantinus, in the same way, fled the fighting,
that crafty man homed to his north country,
the hoary old soldier had nothing to sing of,
the clash of weapons had robbed him of kinsmen,
of friends who fell at the field of battle,
slain in the strife. He had left his own son
young to the sword, on that slaughtering ground,
wounded and maimed. Not much for the greybeard
to sing praise of in that sword-work,
the old fraud, nor for Anlaf either.
With his army lost, no reason to laugh
that they were the better in deeds of war,
in collision of banners on the battle field,
in the spear thrusts, the meeting of men
and trading of blows, when in that blood-test
they played with the offspring of Eadward.

So the Northmen departed in their nailed ships.
Sad leavings of spears, and shamed in their spirits,
they sailed from Dingesmere over deep waters,
seeking Dublin Bay again and Ireland.
In the same way the brothers, both together,
the king and the prince, sought out their kin
in the West Saxon lands, wild with their winning.
They left behind a scattering of corpses,
for the dark ones, for the black raven

with its horned beak, and for the dusky eagle
with its white back, for that greedy war-hawk,
a carrion feast, and for the wild grey beast,
the wolf in the woods.
                         There was never more killing,
on this island, never before so many cut down
by the sword's edge. Never so many bodies,
the old books say, the wise old rememberers,
not since Angles and Saxons came from the east
over the brimming sea, looking for Britain,
and, bold men, war-smiths, eager for glory,
smashed the Welshmen, and battened on this earth.

2. The Death of Alfred; from the *Anglo-Saxon Chronicle*

1036. In this year Alfred, the innocent prince, son of King Aethelred,
came into the country and wished to go to his mother who was living
at Winchester, but Godwin did not permit him to do this, nor the other
barons, because—wrong as it was—sentiment had swung to Harold.

So Godwin seized the young prince and put him in prison.
The retinue he destroyed, found various ways to kill them:
some were sold for cash, some cut down cruelly,
some put in fetters, some were blinded,
some hamstrung, and some of them scalped.
No bloodier deed was ever done in this land,
not since the Danes came and made peace here.
Now it's to be believed that the hands of God
have put them in bliss with Jesus Christ,
for they were guiltless and wretchedly slain.
The Prince was kept alive, threatened by every evil,
until, under advisement, they led him
as they had bound him to Ely-in-the-Fens.

As soon as he landed, he was blinded,
right there on shipboard, hastily,
and blinded he was brought to the monks
and he dwelled there as long as he lived
and afterwards he was buried, as befitted him,
very worthily, for he was a worthy man,
at the west end of the chapel, very near the steeple,
under the church porch. His soul is with Christ.

WHAT THE MODERNISTS WROTE ABOUT:
AN INFORMAL SURVEY

Hart Crane wrote about a bridge, and gulls in the dawn light,
And a subway tunnel, trains plowing through it in the ratcheting dark,
And the hobo camps along the railroad tracks in Indiana
And the flower of a sailor's sex flowering
And the sweet terror of vertical longing in the horse latitudes.

And Thomas Stearns Eliot, poor Tom, as his friends said,
With his brilliance and his prim, squeamish Southern childhood
Channeled Baudelaire and wrote a poem
About sexual hunger and crippling self-consciousness
That made him very famous and refocused European poetry for several
    generations
And then, after his mentor
Bertrand Russell had slept with his—Eliot's—distraught wife,
He wrote a poem—"Mr. Appollinax"—about a philosophical satyr
And then a poem about a broken world and the terrible power
Of spring, numbness after a brutal war, and the bodies
Of working class girls washed up in the Thames
And the boredom and hysteria in the boudoirs of the well-off,
And the memory of a riverside church—some old idea of "inexplicable
    splendor"—
And his desire to die to his sensual life
And later the memory of the laughter of children in a garden
On a path that seemed to lead somewhere indistinct
And probably irrecoverable
And later again the bombs that fell like tongues of flame on London.

Ezra Pound wrote about a number of subjects, as I recall,
Medieval Italian banking and the Paris Metro,
Among them. Also Chinese history

And being imprisoned in a cage,
And the mob that strung his hero Mussolini from a lamppost in Milan,
And when he was younger his first taste of Venice
While he sat on the Dogana's steps,
And he wrote about a woman he remembered—"As cool as the pale, wet
    leaves of lily-of-the-valley"—
Who lay beside him in the dawn.

And Hilda Doolittle saw the Egyptian god Amon
In the green fields of Pennsylvania where he shone
Like the angels she needed to summon to survive the way the violence
Of the devastation of the bombed out city had shaken her and the way,
As a girl, desire had shaken her, and the rhythms of Sappho.

Robinson Jeffers wrote about the Big Sur headlands
And the hawk's beak, and the tidal surges of the sea, and pelicans cruising
Like laden bombers down the coast near Point Pinos.

And Marianne Moore wrote the greatest poem
About a mountain in the twentieth century and called it "An Octopus."
After that, or simultaneously, she wrote a poem about marriage,
The avoidance thereof. And the pangolin and the chambered nautilus
And the exacting work of a steeple jack
In a seaside town where a certain precision of craft
Was a matter of life and death.

                    And Bill Williams,
As his friends called the doctor, except Ezra Pound who called him
Ole Doc Williams, even when they were young,
Wrote about noticing a thirteen year old girl at the curb
On a street corner waiting for the light to change
And glancing down self-consciously at her new breasts,
A quite different take on the subject from Eliot's,
And a girl cutting her little brother's hair by a window

On a summer afternoon in a neighborhood of brick tenements.
And Brueghel, and wild onions, he wrote about, and the way cities burned
Like Christmas greens in the fireplace as the world war churned on.
And about how the coming of spring to a bare winter field
In New Jersey resembled the violence of child birth
And how he was disgusted with himself for being sexually attracted
To the half-witted girl who helped clean their house.

And Wallace Stevens wrote about the Connecticut River
And an early winter snowfall in Hartford
And the way sexual magic dissipated in his life
And what his Pennsylvania Dutch mother would think of his pretty
And explicitly atheist poems—
"Ach, mutter," he wrote, "this old, black dress,
I have been embroidering French flowers on it"—
And the nature of imagination, and something
About the fact that you can regard blackbirds
From several points of view.

And Lola Ridge wrote about the New York ghetto
In something like the way Langston Hughes wrote about the Harlem
    streets
Because he perhaps took his manner at first from her
And from Carl Sandburg and, listening to the blues,
Made it his own when he described the rent parties
And the suicides and the grifters, the lovers, the numbers runners,
And the "boogie-woogie rumble of a dream deferred."

And Mina Loy wrote about sex that was like pigs rooting,
Also, more fastidiously, the vowel sounds produced by a contemplation of
    the moon.

And Gertrude Stein. About was a writing. Outwardly. It was exceedingly
    about.

A TALK AT SEWANEE

Ellen Douglas who is dead now—
She must have been eighty that year
And would live for another decade,

Though she never wrote another novel
And had just published a book called *Truth*,
Four Stories I Am Finally Old Enough to Tell—

Was wearing a pair of jeans, got away,
Some of the young women remarked later,
With wearing a pair of jeans and a shirt

Of light, peach-colored linen in the July heat,
By which they meant it was not some undignified
Gesture toward girlishness. She wore what she wore

Well, and center stage, arms crossed, seated on a stool
In front of a room full of reverent young Southerners
Wore an expression on her face that seemed to me—

I am consulting my old journals—both "baffled
And completely self-assured." It was a face
To which you still wanted to attach the word "pretty,"

Not feminine, but womanly, or adult and female,
And the shimmer of chestnut in her grey hair,
Was pleasant to look at. "Style," she was saying,

"Is really just seeing. It's the way they talk about
A way of seeing. If you want to write, read,
And if you read good books well, it will wake in you

A desire to say what you mean. At least it did
In me. The things that you read that matter to you,
The things they call your influences, are the books
That introduce you to yourself, and they will lead,
Or ought to, to a patient persistent attempt
To say what you mean." Another note reads:
"You have to write blind to eventually see clearly
What your subject is." A close, humid room
In the middle of Tennessee in the middle of July.
Outside you could not tell if the green hum
In the old live oaks was generating the insect buzz
Or the buzz was generating the green humming
In the air that was indistinguishable,
When you walked in it, from the soaked
Odor of the summer grass. I was an outsider
To what I took to be this transaction in heritage.
Her authority, I knew, derived from the ten
Or so novels and books of stories she'd written
Over the course of thirty years. She had written
About whiteness in Mississippi from the point of view
Of what race and gender relations did to the lives
Of women inside families and that she must have got
It right, or some of it right, I thought I could tell
From the palpable silence and the leaning-forward bodies
Of the young writers in that otherwise uncomfortable room,
Fanning themselves with their manuscripts or conference schedules
Like spectators fanning in Southern courtrooms in the movies.
I had been thinking that day of my cousin Lisa's death
From an overdose of drugs. It's brutal, the way some lives
Seem to work and some don't. She was twenty-nine,
She'd acquired a taste for heroin at sixteen
From her nineteen year old boyfriend who was the son
Of a record company executive in L.A. They went
To the same private school. Lisa was my playmate

Summers in the early years of our childhoods,
The runt of her litter of three brothers, part pest,
Part loved kid sister, and a very funny person,
A risk-taker to keep up with and provoke her brothers.
At sixteen I remember that both she and her boyfriend
Wore black leather jackets and that she had pinned
To hers the dried up body of a large flattened toad
She'd found in the street and apparently identified with.
She'd married, had a child, been in and out
Of expensive treatment programs that her older brother
Who we called Skipper had also been in and out of
Because of the drinking problem he must have gotten sick of.
Skipper jumped the year before from a highway overpass
Into the middle of the commute hour traffic in Pasadena.
I called my aunt, who would have been the old writer's age.
She said, "You know, I have no tears. Isn't that awful. I
Seem to be out of tears." Ellen Douglas is a pen name.
Born in the 1920s into a world in which respectability
Could have pressed her into collusion with a degrading
System of apartheid. I don't know what saves people.
I know we tend to love our children. I know addiction
Wrecks lives. It feels like a mystery, whatever idea
Of the good had set that handsome old woman
In front of the audience of young writers, shaking
Her head, saying, "You have to write your way
To knowing what you have to say, and then,
With no guarantees, you have to keep trying
To write your way in the general direction
Of what it would feel like to actually say it."

THE FOUR ETERNITIES,
OR THE GRANDFATHER'S TALE

"Tell me a story about a princess," she said.
One whose hair is blond? One whose hair is red?
"One whose hair is black and very, very curly."
Well, it was early in the time called once upon a time
And a young girl whose hair was very, very black.
"And curly." And curly, lived high in the mountains
Near a great blue lake. And on this particular day
She was up very early because her hair was a problem.
It took forever to brush it. And she couldn't rush it.
She was the king's trapper's daughter, and—"I thought,"
She said, "that this was a story about a princess."
And so it will be. But on that day because it was early
Because her hair was so very, very curly and because
She had tasks she really ought to perform, the king's
Trapper's daughter. "What is a trapper?" she asked.
A trapper is a man whose task it is to trap small animals,
So kings and queens can dress in furs. And on that day
She needed her hair to be in some semblance of array
Because there were tasks a king's trapper's daughter
Ought to be performing. There were ermine skins
To cure and fox skins and the skins of badgers
And of stoats. "What do you cure a fox skin of?"
She asked. Being alive. Her father had several boats
And he had taken one of them across the blue lake
Because sometimes kings and queens needed the hair
Of a bear to warm their beds or to keep from their feet
The chill of the stones on the palace floor. There was more
For the girl with the black, black hair to do
In a day than a story like this can properly say,
But one of the things she had absolutely to do

Was gather the roots to mix the tanning water.
"What's tanning water?" She was the king's trapper's
Daughter and one of her chores by the great blue lake,
The lake whose blue was the icy blue of the bluest ice,
Was to gather the roots, lots and lots and lots and lots
Of elderberry and gooseberry roots and the human-shaped roots
Of the mountain lilies to make the water to soak the furs
Of the ermine and the badger and the fox and the stoat
That made them fluffy and shiny and made them last
Past the life of any single king or queen. There were furs
That could be seen on the backs of the most beautiful princesses
For several generations. To release their shininess,
The furs had to be teased and squeezed in the tanning water
By the king's trapper's daughter, and that was why,
In a world full of whys and sighs and reasons for things,
The fine, small hands of the king's trapper's daughter
Were dyed a bright royal purple. "I think I'm going
To go to sleep now," she said. All right, my darling.
You go to sleep now, sweetness, and tomorrow
When it is still early in the once upon a time time
We can listen to more of the story of the great blue lake
And the girl whose hair was very, very black.
"Just very black," she said. "Very, very curly."

SILENCE

For Ursula Le Guin, 1929–2018

They descended through a steep defile, she first,
delicately, breasting the thick air like a swan
in muddy water, he following. They had both
known the red spider story in which death
made its vow to silence, so they had not spoken
since leaving the valley of moths, and one polyphemus
the color of shagbark, with large purplish spots
on its hindwings like a lemur's eyes, was still fixed
to her shoulder just at the neck and seemed
to be staring at him. The rope bridge swayed
when they traversed the chasm. He went swiftly,
leaping from strand to thick strand, and across
he pulled hard to make the handrails taut,
and though it still swung violently as she crossed,
she paused halfway to let the spray of the cataract
cool her and then finished in long strides
as if she were still climbing the almost vertical
jade stairs to the temple commons. They paused
to share a mango, the juices dribbling golden
from her chin to her breast which made him smile
and she, examining the moth whose proboscis
was probing the follicle of one of her neck hairs
as it folded and unfolded its wings in flickers
of what seemed sexual intentness, brushed it off
and the creature rose, circled her once, twice, and floated
down the canyon. From there the path was well marked,
soft with pine needles in the forest and a wide swatch
of road lined with the deep ruts of wagon wheels,

through the savannah. The wind blew east to west,
so their scent was behind them, and the large cats,
if they trailed them, kept their distance, and,
except for some few languid cries that night
when they lay under the huge glittering field
of the stars, they heard no trace of them, and,
still not speaking to one another, walking
with that same nearly identical rhythmic gait,
she first through the morning, he in the afternoon,
they came to the pavilion before sundown,
where they bathed, burnt an offering of herbs,
were given a light meal, and when the sun had set
entered the hall for the first of the old woman's lectures
on the color of vowels. She entered the room
quite casually though with her characteristic grace,
greeted some of the novices, knelt facing the audience,
shook out her white hair and sat very still
for what seemed a long time before they could hear,
emanating from deep in her diaphragm
the humming sound that signified the letter *a*.
The light in the room deepened to that shade
Of mauve adduced from the story of the color
of the mourning garment that the old queen wore
for the boy who had had the bad luck to arouse
her attention; adduced also from the legend about the origin
of the color on the throat of the green-backed thrushes
that visited the islands in the spring whose songs
were said to be so inconsolable that they were imitated
only by the monks who tended the temple-without-images
which was dedicated to the gods of faceless longing.

(They absorbed the sweetness and the terror of it,
but did not join in the humming which they felt,
their vow aside, belonged to her and to her stillness.)

THE SIXTH SHEIKH'S SHEEP'S SICK

Praise to the breath, and the lips, and the teeth.
Praise to the tongue and to the larynx and the pharynx
And the soft palate and the hard palate and the vibration
Of the vocal cords. Peter Piper picked a peck
Of sea shells by the sea shore. She sells rubber
Baby buggy bumpers. It's early March, late
Afternoon. There's one tiny tufted titmouse
In the bare branches of the sycamore just outside
My window. The smallest and the loudest
Of all the spring birds. Its eye the size
Of a single black currant. Three sweet notes,
Perfectly spaced, and then sometimes four.
Not difficult to say "one tiny tufted titmouse,"
But it requires a small increment of effort,
And "in the bare branches of the sycamore"
Is pure pleasure. When I read my poems aloud,
I find it's hard to say that the people "stand
On tiptoe to pick ripe huckleberries that the deer
Can't reach." Pick ripe huckleberries. Aluminum
Linoleum. The round leaf buds on the tips
Of the branches of the sycamore are glowing
Gold in the afternoon sun. Three sweet notes
Again. It wants a mate. Maybe. Maybe it's
Just playing. Researchers have taught chimps
Over a hundred words and the books say
They can't use them to form new concepts.
She sells pickled peppers. Three notes again!
But "can't" doesn't seem quite right. What
If it's just not in the range of things
They want to do. I want to say "ripe huckleberries,"
"The titmouse flits from branch to branch,"

Because I want to. Praise to the breath,
And the teeth, and the lips. Praise to the tongue,
And to the animal who first said "pharynx,"
And to the one who first said "larynx," praise.

Life hasn't mainly to do
with man, still less with ideas.
What is it then that life has to
do with?

Maybe someone knows, Eugenio Montale wrote,
In the Arrowsmith translation, but his lips are sealed
And he's not saying. In his notebooks.
He must have been eighty years old.
One day he wrote about reading Cavafy,
Something about Nero taking a nap,
What a beautiful man he was, how,
Hearing the howling of the Furies,
His household gods must have crept away
While he was sleeping. And then—elliptical
Montale—he writes, *I am the emperor*
Of nothing. I don't even own
A mousetrap. Another day he writes
About a Jehovah's Witness at the door.
Which is more frightening, the idea that the world
Ends in a cataclysm or the idea
That it doesn't? And the day after that
He is thinking about the character of the transvestite
In old Italian melodrama. We don't really need makeup,
He says, all we have to do
Is look in the mirror to see that we're someone else.
So many years of living when we had sensations
And not opinions. Now, he writes, even children
In grade school have opinions. (This was in the 1970s.)
It can come to be a question of what you want

From poetry. Think of an eight year old boy in 1905
On a hot summer day in the market square
In some little Ligurian town (on a hilltop,
Swifts swooping across the sky between the church tower
And the city hall) having his first taste
Of a grape-flavored cone of crushed ice.
Before there were opinions. Some years ago
A woman, a poet whose work I had read
And admired, invited me to lunch. She was a busy person
And so it was a distinct kindness. I went to her office—
It was summer—and she'd laid out a picnic
On her desk. Grapes, goat cheese in little rounds,
Pickles, a local bread (this was in New England
In the 1970s, Montale would have been alive
Still) and we nibbled, and talked and talked.
I think we even had a glass of wine. Later I came
To have reservations about her poems or—not so much her poems
As her attitude toward poetry—what it was that bothered me
I don't even remember—and later still we'd meet occasionally
At literary events in New York or Boston
And would be distantly cordial when there had been
Between us this intimacy of having been young
And having loved unreservedly this art
We were still discovering. I had the news yesterday
That she's in a coma, having had a massive stroke.
I know that people do recover and I can only hope.
I don't know much about her life. A long marriage,
Children. I imagine she was an intensely present mother,
Present given the fact that she was a poet.
I don't know if she felt she had accomplished
Her art. A friend came to the door recently
And said why don't we get stoned and write a poem together?
And I had things on my mind and said no.
We don't live altogether in either opinions

Or sensations or in some mix of the two
Like the fast succession of scenes
In Nero's afternoon nap. For what that is
I think Husserl invented the term *lebenswelt*.
After my friend left, staring at the blank page of a journal
In which I'd been writing, I first felt terrible
And then tried to think about what line of poetry
Or idea of a line of poetry I could present to Montale
In the Jehovah's Witness heaven after the catastrophe
When it all looked, from that distance,
Like a Sunday band concert in an Italian town
At the turn of the nineteenth century.
Or could have presented to my friend to remind her
Of how we had loved the very idea of the line.
Maybe *it rained yesterday, and the evening air was cool.*
Or loved the simplest enjambment in a pair of lines.
Maybe, *we walked to the waterfall. On the way*
There was a patch of mountain lilies. And
Loved how a few lines made a flowing. Maybe
The mother bear leapt onto the trunk of a fallen tree
To look back at us, or more probably to sniff us out.
And seemed to decide we were not a problem,
And came down off her perch in an easy cascade
Of brown fur, and disappeared into the forest.

SMALL ACT OF HOMAGE

Reading Sophie Laffitte's biography of Chekhov
    —what an admirable life!—
    in a café in the international lounge
    at Mexico City airport—
and, just as, in the last chapter,
he is dying, a waiter appears,
a middle-aged man with an Olmec face,
    bearing a beautifully foamy cappuccino,
    the milk foam dripping down the sides
    of the white ceramic cup.
I licked it off slowly for Chekhov.

———

Reading Sophie Laffitte's biography of Chekhov
    —what an admirable life!—
in the café in the international lounge
    of the Mexico City airport—
and just as he is dying in the last chapter
    a waiter appears, a middle-aged man
with a solemn Olmec face—Chekhov
would have known his age, how his two sons
    were employed, how he had achieved
the particular dignity and indifference
with which he served me a beautifully foamy cappuccino,
    the bubbles of milk foam
dripping down the sides of the white ceramic cup.
I kept reading and licked it off slowly.

———

Reading Sophie Laffitte's biography of Chekhov
    in a café in the international lounge
    at Mexico City airport—
and, just as, in the last chapter,
he is dying, a waiter appears,
    bearing a beautifully foamy cappuccino,
    the milk foam dripping down the sides
    of the white ceramic cup.
I licked it off for Chekhov.

NOTES ON THE NOTION OF A BOUNDLESS POETICS

for Lyn Hejinian

Pierre Reverdy: All talk of poetics is more or less indiscreet praise of one's own methods.

But why not? Who is going to defend or explain, or for that matter take an interest in them, if the poet doesn't?

My first response to the phrase "boundless poetics" was to imagine putting on an old phonograph a 78 rpm recording of Mississippi John Hurt singing "Make Me a Pallet on the Floor" and lying down on the floor and listening to it.

Down, pretty baby, soft and low.

And then maybe getting up and putting on the Lucinda Williams version from *Ramblin'*.

I think it might be the election. The word "boundless" calling up immediately the rhetorics of American exceptionalism. It makes me want a presidential candidate who would promise to make the United States the fourth richest country in the world, one that would take care of its elderly and of people who are struggling in their lives, and would try to learn from other countries, and would pay its dues to the United Nations promptly and gratefully.

The second thing that came to mind was a one line poem by Czesław Miłosz entitled "On the need to draw boundaries." It goes, in its entirety, "Wretched and dishonest was the sea." In an English translation of the word order of the original, except that there is no "the" in Polish.

"Pallet," according to the *OED* is a very old word, came into English from medieval French in which a *paillet* was a bundle of straw. Chaucer's *Troilus:* "On a paylet / all that glad night by Troilus he lay."

There have probably never been more means available to poets, ever, in the history of the written art in English than there are now. From intricate rhymed and metrical forms to prose to concrete poems, audio poems, video poems. Perhaps not infinite means, but lots.

And in that sense, I guess, one could speak of a boundless poetics. And— but—to choose to do any one thing is to choose not to do everything else you might have done instead and in that sense any poetics, any making, is bounded. So maybe *sustainable* poetics? An *adequate* poetics?

Connected in my mind somehow with manners. Politeness, consideration, civility. Some Swiss canton of the mind where the inhabitants practice an externalized disposition to kindness.

But also connected to what is one of the most thrilling things to me about an art or work of art—the way it traverses and embodies the energy of a gesture.

And gesture, like energy, in humans, is finite. And in a particular work of art finite also, but you might say, infinitely finite: done with and ongoing. Pound, Olson: poem as hieroglyph, etc.

The third thing that came to my mind was to wonder why the first thing that came to my mind was a lyric in which the speaker is a man who wants a woman's body very badly and understands that to act on his desire would be a betrayal. Something about an intensity of need that drives you to your knees. How a poetics might imply it.

And I love Bashō, so I am not drawn to the poetics of extremity. Bashō would think the impulse vulgar. (Nabokov: *poshlost.*) A hard November

rain after a stretch of mild autumnal days. Foaming gutters the color
of potato skins, raindrops leaping off hard metal in a parking lot. One
of those gusts of breath off the Pacific. He would have been satisfied
to get that into language. And it wasn't exactly mimesis he was after,
though he was certainly committed to a mimetic tradition. (Here a
notion of manners comes in—what might be thought of as the basis of an
ecopoetics, a courtesy.)

But representing an external world is not quite what he meant when he
said "Learn about bamboo from the bamboo."

The fourth thing that came to mind was the notion that obsession had the
virtue of combining quite narrow boundaries and boundlessness. Eugenio
Montale: *Per qualche anno ho dipinto solo ròccoli*. A *ròccolo* is a bird-trap.

A lashing Pacific storm. Like the crack of a whip or a temperamental
prince. The native peoples of this coast must have had myth names for
kinds of storms, they must have had stories! Lower Manhattan in flood
and the need to draw boundaries. A gasp in cold air.

There are probably lots of procedures to set a piece of writing in motion,
a seriality that proposes no limit and that would be, in that sense,
boundless, but it would seem, it always seems, to end up as a form, a
footrace between the narcissism of the writer and the attention span of
the reader or auditor. Or between the writer's diligence and the reader's
patience. Still a "boundless" poetics (i.e., he does "go on," doesn't he?)
and if the writer is having a good time, why not?

My own stumbling a desire for lightness, and also necessity like a metallic
taste in the mouth, and the civility of shape.

And I think of Gorky's story about Tolstoy in Yalta grabbing him by the
back of the neck with his great hand and pointing his head toward an old
woman picking rags in the street across from the café where they were

having lunch with Chekhov. They had been talking about writing. And Tolstoy, he said, held his head and said "Her, her."

So there is writing and there are ideas about it and the world full of rain, so many parts of it either tragic or brutal, any sense of responsibility to which would be a boundary as well as an entry.

And time as a boundary, e.g., the telephone just rang. Writing this I was missing a meeting.

Notes

An Argument: As I hope is clear, the words spoken by Czesław Miłosz in this poem are my words, not his. They are about an argument in my head—I suppose I should say the poem's narrator's head—that reflects and condenses years of conversation. He spoke often of the danger and the arbitrariness of survival in the years of the German occupation of Warsaw and once of being stopped for a jacket he was wearing. The exact story as narrated in the poem he did not tell me. That belongs to the poem's narrator's imagination of his experience. Similarly he mentioned having tea with Lunia Czechowska in Paris. The details belong to the narrator's imagination.

The Archaeology of Plenty: I borrowed the title from Anne Cheng.

A Person Should: My son Leif is a physician and works in hospitals that are about equidistant from the university and the neighborhoods of the urban poor. He's remarked to me on the experience of trying to comfort elderly professors, often European, often figures of considerable authority in their worlds, who have been reduced to hospital gowns and frightening diagnoses or to the waiting rooms where families cope as they can with illness and death. The woman in this poem is a composite figure, based on two separate acquaintances and experiences.

Smoking in Heaven: For decaffeinated time, cf. Brenda Hillman, "Time Problem," *Loose Sugar* (Wesleyan University Press, 1997).

For Cecil: C. S. Giscombe, *Ohio Railroads* (Omnidawn, 2014).

Large Bouquet: Chen Li is an enormously inventive Taiwanese poet who was kind enough to translate some of my poems into Mandarin. Being aware that you might be translated, I find, makes you look at your own words differently.

Nature Notes 2: The phrase "all awash with angels" belongs to Richard Wilbur and his poem "Love Calls Us to the Things of This World."

After Xue Di: Xue Di, *Across Borders,* translated by Alison Friedman (Green Integer, 2014).

Dancing: For the account of the history of the Kalashnikov, I am indebted to the work of C. J. Chivers in the *New York Times,* February 15, 2018.

Seoul Notebook: A record of this conference can be found at *Writing for Peace: Proceedings of the 2nd Seoul International Forum for Literature 2005,* ed. Uchang Kim (University of Hawaii Press, 2011). I did not consult the print version of the talks. I was trying to catch my experience as an auditor rather than make a faithful account of the proceedings. And I've fictionalized Holly and her family a little to preserve their privacy.

A Talk at Sewanee: The words spoken by the novelist Ellen Douglas in this poem are taken from my notes on her craft talk with students. I had no text of hers to check for accuracy, but I hope I caught the spirit of it, if I did not get it word for word.

Acknowledgments

Thanks to the editors of the publications in which the following poems first appeared:

"Christmas in August," *Saveur*

"Abbott's Lagoon: October," *Bay Nature*

"Planh or Dirge for the Ones Who Die in Their Thirties," *West Marin Review*

"An Argument About Poetics Imagined at Squaw Valley After a Night Walk Under the Mountain," *Literary Imagination*

"Second Person," *Berkeley Poetry Review*

"Nature Notes" and "Summer Storm in the Sierra," *Zyzzyva*

"First Poem," *Ploughshares*

"The Four Eternities," "Three Dreams About Buildings," "Dream in the Summer of My Seventy-Third Year," and "Three Propositions About a Subject Still to Be Determined," *Jung Journal*

"Dancing" first appeared in *Bullets into Bells: Poets and Citizens Respond to Gun Violence*, ed. Brian Clements, Alexandra Teague, and Dean Rader (Beacon Press, 2017). It was also printed in the *American Poetry Review* and *West Marin Review* and reprinted in *Pushcart Prize XLII: Best of the Small Presses* (2018).

"Sunglasses Billboard in Termini Station" appeared in *Poems of Rome*, ed. Karl Kirchwey (Everyman's Library, 2018).

"To Be Accompanied by Flute and Zither" first appeared in *Fire and Rain: Ecopoetry from California*, ed. Lucille Lang Day and Ruth Nolan

(Scarlet Tanager Books, 2018). "Abbott's Lagoon: October" was also reprinted there.

"A Person Should," "After Xue Di," "Cymbeline," "For Cecil, After Reading *Ohio Railroads*," "Hotel Room," and "The Poet at Nine" appeared in *Berlin Quarterly*.

"Pertinent Divigations Toward an Ode to Inuit Carvers," "The Sixth Sheikh's Sheep's Sick," "Notes on the Notion of a Boundless Poetics," and "Harvest" appeared in *Lana Turner*.

"Creech Notebook: Drones in the Desert," appeared in *Kenyon Review*

"Poem Not an Elegy in a Season of Elegies" and "Silence," appeared in *Catamaran*

I've mostly assembled books of poems as a solitary occupation. This time I've had reason to be grateful to many friends for their good eyes and ears and for their friendship. Deep thanks to Norma Cole, Saskia Hamilton, Rob Kaufman, Jesse Nathan, Jack Shoemaker, and Matthew Zapruder. I am especially grateful to John Shoptaw for his close reading of the manuscript. And to the ones, over many years, who have to my great good fortune made the work less solitary: Brenda Hillman, for sharing a life and her imagination (which age cannot wither nor custom stale); and my editor and friend, Dan Halpern, without whose encouragement I would very likely never have got a book together.